A PLACE FOR REVELATION

ALBERT SCHWEITZER

A PLACE FOR REVELATION

Sermons on
Reverence for Life

TRANSLATED BY
David Larrimore Holland

MACMILLAN PUBLISHING COMPANY *New York*

COLLIER MACMILLAN PUBLISHERS *London*

Emmy Martin and Martin Strege
IN MEMORIAM

Published in German as *Was Sollen Wir Tun?*, copyright © 1986 by Verlag Lambert Schneider GmbH—Heidelberg

Scripture quotations from the Revised Standard Version Bible © 1946, 1952, 1971, by the Division of Christian Education of the National Council of the Churches of Christ in the United States of America. Used by permission.

Scripture quotations from the New English Bible © The Delegates of the Oxford University Press and the Syndics of the Cambridge University Press, 1961, 1970. Reprinted by permission.

Macmillan Publishing Company
866 Third Avenue, New York, NY 10022
Collier Macmillan Canada, Inc.

Library of Congress Cataloging-in-Publication Data
Schweitzer, Albert, 1875–1965.
   [Was sollen wir tun? English]
   A place for revelation: sermons on reverence for life/Albert Schweitzer; translated by David Larrimore Holland.
      p. cm.
   Translation of: Was sollen wir tun?
   ISBN 0-02-607811-2
   1. Sermons, English—Translations from German.   2. Sermons, German—Translations into English.   I. Title.
   BV4254.G3S3313   1988
   252—dc19   88-21611   CIP

Macmillan books are available at special discounts for bulk purchases for sales promotions, premiums, fund-raising, or educational use. For details, contact:

   Special Sales Director
   Macmillan Publishing Company
   866 Third Avenue
   New York, N.Y. 10022

10 9 8 7 6 5 4 3 2 1
Printed in the United States of America

Contents

Contents

Translator's Preface

Translating Albert Schweitzer's *Was Sollen Wir Tun?* has been a joy as well as a labor. Not everything I have hitherto translated for publication has moved me to rethink my own apprehensions in an area of life as persuasively as do these twelve sermons of Schweitzer. I hope they will find a wide readership in their English garb, for theirs is a potent message that is quite as timely today as it was at the end of World War I.

For the most part, the task of rendering Schweitzer's German into English has not been onerous. Only on three occasions have I felt it necessary to add a note to his text in explanation of a feature of the German that could not find equivalence in English. Schweitzer's texts were not always what he actually said to his congregations verbatim, but apparently served him as foils for a more direct sort of communication of his message. That means that upon occasion, especially in those sermons in which the conclusion exists only in outline form, but also in parts of his main texts, Schweitzer's thoughts have tumbled one upon the other without the more expansive expositions one might have anticipated. But the message is vivid nevertheless. And vital!

I should like to take this opportunity to dedicate this translation to some close friends whose help during the past year has been more significant to me than they realize. They are Eric and Mousie, Jane and Brian, Molly and Bobby, John and Mimi, Carolyn, Frances, and my very best friend and companion, my wife, Jill.

Easter Day, 1988   D.L.H.

Foreword to the New Edition

The book *Was Sollen Wir Tun?* (What Ought We to Do?) came into being in the following manner. Martin Strege, at the beginning of the 1970s, found transcripts of the preaching cycle of 1919 in the central archive of Günsbach and gathered them together into a first manuscript. It proved necessary, however, to compare the text with the handwritten manuscripts, which were for the most part still extant. That task then devolved upon Lothar Stiehm, who prepared the definitive text and the commentary for the first edition of the book, which appeared in 1974.

For the present new printing in the "lambert schneider taschenbücher" (Lambert Schneider Pocketbooks) series, the text was improved and expanded in certain places on the basis of another examination of the original manuscript. . . .

Martin Strege, who had been active in his Pomeranian homeland as a pastor for a long time (up until his expulsion in 1945), died in 1976. He had joined in numerous publications for Schweitzer's theological and philosophical positions over a period of several decades and was, from 1928 onward, a true friend of the doctor's. The dedication of the new printing includes the memorial to Martin Strege: his heart was set on the publication of these sermons.

Heidelberg, Autumn 1985   L.S.

A Word Beforehand

July 1918: A man comes home from internment.

The year 1913; Good Friday afternoon; Albert Schweitzer had set out with his wife for Lambarene: first work in the primeval forest of Central Africa. Nevertheless, already on August 5, 1914, a year later, the news comes: There is war in Europe! "Already on the evening of that day we received the advice that we were to regard ourselves as prisoners. . . ." Service in the hospital is forbidden to the "foreign enemy."

That pushes forward a question Schweitzer had been carrying around with him for years: *How can we people live in a culture that is worthy of mankind?* Work begins on the "Philosophy of Culture," still without progress until 1915, when the key phrase of his thought occurs to him: *reverence for life.*

The first sketches remain behind when Helene and Albert Schweitzer are evacuated. Schweitzer entrusts the manuscript "to the American missionary Ford, who was working at that time in Lambarene. He [Ford]—as he confessed to me—would have preferred to throw the heavy package into the river, because he regarded philosophy as unnecessary and even injurious. . . ."

Then comes life imprisoned from camp to camp: in

the *caserne de passage* (the transitional barracks) in Bordeaux, in Garaison, in the old Pyrennian monastery, in Saint Rémy in Provence. Shortly before, this monastery had been a lunatic asylum: van Gogh's drawing captured the high, bleak space with the iron oven and the long pipe. . . . Finally: in exchange back to Alsace, return to his native Günsbach.

His *native* Günsbach—?

Günsbach lay in a zone of military operations. The muffled rumble of artillery shots from the mountains. Battered homes all around. Bald hills! The worry bore heavily. "A terrible dryness reigned. The grain dried out; potatoes sticking out. On many meadows the grass was so thin it didn't pay to mow it. From their stalls the bellowing of hungry cows resounded. If a storm appeared on the horizon, it passed without yielding any rain . . . only wind that sucked the earth dry of every last bit of moisture, and clouds of dust, in which strode the specter of hunger."

The man, sick with a fever—weakened by dysentery since Bordeaux—drags himself along the road to Colmar until he can find a way to ride. On September 1, 1918, Schweitzer undergoes surgery in Strasbourg.

Thereafter, a groping toward a new beginning. Who here wants to know anything of him? Like a penny rolled under the furniture and lost!

Thanks to a kindly intercession, he becomes assistant physician at the City Hospital and at the same time vicar of Saint Nicolai (the parish church with which he had been entrusted earlier and which stood across from Saint Thomas): Now at least he knows where his living will come from.

From this period come the texts in our volume: no routine Sunday sermons these! This is a man who had experienced something with himself and with the world and who had reflected about that—seeking, doubting, hoping. Simple expressions. Themes from daily life. As the old Christian Adam Dann, the *spiritus rector* of the third sermon of this volume, the "animal sermon," says: "Whoever torments animals will torment people; from animal murderers come people murderers, unawares—and profaners of God." It is basically a matter of the small acts. *There* is decided what happens in the world in one's larger actions. The core ideas of his own philosophy, thought out in Africa, Schweitzer here addresses for the first time to other people.

In the summer of 1919, Schweitzer has again to undergo surgery. Sermons eleven and twelve are written in the surgical hospital, and were written out in a weak hand. Conscientious answers concerning daily questions that are important to him.

At the end of 1919 comes the saving invitation of Archbishop Nathan Söderblom to deliver the Olaus Petri Lectures at the University of Uppsala (concerning the fundamental ideas of his philosophy). Armed with letters of recommendation, Schweitzer travels throughout the land afterward, giving organ concerts and lectures. From the proceeds he can finally pay his debts and finally save for a second trip to Lambarene in order to begin anew. Life challenges him again. So he is unable to carry forward the "Ethical Sermons" any longer. Piece after piece of our existence was to have been treated in the same manner. In the penultimate of these sermons, the one written in hospital, there is a marginal note: "The bells are just ringing in peace, on the 23rd of June, 1919, at 9:15."

. . . peace?

How many wars have been fought on earth since

then? As I write these lines (October 1973), there rages in the Sinai desert—a place of God's revelation and law-giving—one of the largest tank battles in the history of warfare. Begun on Yom Kippur, the Day of Atonement. . . .

Was sollen wir tun? The questions this man posed then on the threshold from war to peace have remained till today—only a few timely expressions need be changed. *The answers remain, too.* Schweitzer's answers are plain, but they follow one challengingly—until the point where the voice in you speaks. Quiet, steadfast earnestness. No routine Sunday sermons. No ideological phrases that make things simplistic. But simple *answers*, expressions from man to man, for me and for you.

L.S.

Twelve Sermons on Ethical Problems

1. FIRST SERMON ON REVERENCE FOR LIFE

And one of the scribes came up and heard them disputing with one another, and seeing that he answered them well, asked him, "Which commandment is the first of all?" Jesus answered, "The first is, 'Hear, O Israel: The Lord our God, the Lord is one; and you shall love the Lord your God with all your heart, and with all your soul, and with all your mind, and with all your strength.' The second is this, 'You shall love your neighbor as yourself.' There is no commandment greater than these." And the scribe said to him, "You are right, Teacher; you have truly said that he is one, and there is no other but he; and to love him with all the heart, and with all the understanding, and with all the strength, and to love one's neighbor as oneself, is much more than all whole burnt offerings and sacrifices." And when Jesus saw that he answered wisely, he said to him, "You are not far from the kingdom of God." And after that no one dared to ask him any question.

MARK 12:28–34, RSV

Albert Schweitzer

The scribe who poses the question to Jesus about the greatest commandment is eager to learn. He wants information about something that concerns him and many of his comrades. In the Gospel according to Matthew, in chapter 22, the scribes pose this question to Jesus in order to tempt him. But the evangelist Mark surely has the better memory when he describes the congenial encounter in which Jesus and the scribes understand each other for a moment, look into each others' hearts, and then go their separate ways again.

In those days, thinking Israelites were considering the problem of how all of the commandments, both great and small, might be traced back to one basic law. We, too, have a similar need. *What is intrinsic good?* I have read to you the eternal words of our Lord about forgiveness, mercy, love, and all of the other characteristics we as his disciples are to prove true in the world. But we all seem to think of these qualities as only colors refracted from the white light of some basic ethical attitude, such as he requires from us.

I want to reflect with you now on this question: What is this basic ethical attitude? Later on I shall devote several meditations to the questions of Christian ethics upon which I have been ruminating in distant lands, in the isolation of the primeval forest, but always with these services in Saint Nicholai's in mind and in the confident hope of being able someday to speak to you about them.

The question of exactly what this basic ethical attitude might be imposes itself upon us nowadays. We are forced into a recognition that earlier generations and, until recently, even we ourselves refused to accept. We cannot escape it, however, if we want to be truthful: *Christian ethics has never become a power in the world.*

4

It has never penetrated very deeply into the human soul but, rather, has been accepted only superficially, more acknowledged in words than practiced in deeds. Mankind acts as if the words of Jesus did not exist for them, as if there were no ethics for them at all.

That is why it is useless simply to rehearse and interpret the ethical commandments of Jesus again and again, as if that would somehow in the end produce their general acceptance. That would be like painting with beautiful colors on a wet wall. We must first of all create a *foundation for understanding* those commandments and guide our world into a frame of mind in which Jesus' teachings have meaning. And it is by no means easy to interpret the words of Jesus so that they can be used practically in life. For example, let us take the sayings about the greatest of the commandments. What does it mean to love God with all your heart and only to do good out of love for him? Follow up on this idea and a world of considerations opens up before you. When in life have you chosen to do good out of love for God when you otherwise would have chosen to do evil? And take the other commandment: "You should love your neighbor as yourself." Truly, that is wonderful. I could expound it to you in the most charming examples. *But can it be carried through?* Suppose for the moment that, beginning tomorrow, you wanted literally to live according to that commandment. What would the results be in a few days?

That is the greatest riddle in Christian ethical teaching. We cannot simply apply the words of Jesus directly to life, however holy our desire to serve him. And from that comes the great danger that we shall give a respectful reference to Jesus' words and praise them as "ideal" but in reality leave them unnoticed.

Still another misunderstanding endangers the realization of Christian morality. The attempt easily makes us arrogant. If we forgive our enemies, we think ourselves terribly virtuous. If we assist someone who needs our help, we consider ourselves very noble. For in doing the few things that, in the spirit of Christ, we can do differently from and better than other people, we feel ourselves superior to them. This unethical self-satisfaction seems frequently almost to make us more unethical than those who do not even acknowledge the commandments of Jesus or endeavor to follow them. Precisely because they demand something so extraordinary, it is difficult for us to regard the demands of Jesus as *ordinary*. Yet that is precisely what he asks us to do, to see his demands as ordinary. For he says that, however much we have done, we should still regard ourselves as useless servants.

That is why we must think together concerning the intrinsic good. We want to understand how the highly exalted demands of Jesus are to be fulfilled in daily life, and we want to be able to comprehend them, though highly exalted, as the ordinary duty of mankind.

We want to grasp the fundamental principle of all ethics and to derive from that underlying principle, as from a supreme law, all ethical actions. Yes, but can morality be grasped at all? Is it not a matter of the heart? Does it not depend on love? That has been said to us repeatedly for two thousand years. And what is the result?

Let's observe humanity around us, both collectively and individually. Why are people so often unprincipled? Why are even the most pious among them—and often these in particular!—able to let themselves be carried along by prejudice and nationalist passion into judgments and actions that are no longer ethical at all?

Because they lack a morality based on reason and founded logically in reason. Because for them ethics is not something given with reason as a natural endowment.

Reason and the heart must work together if a true morality is to be established. And herein lies the problem for all abstract ethical questions as well as for practical decisions in daily life.

When I say reason, I refer to an understanding that penetrates to the depths of things and that embraces the wholeness of reality, extending even into the realm of the will.

We experience a noteworthy duality when we seek to understand ourselves in light of the ethical will within us. We observe, on the one hand, that the moral will is connected to reason. On the other hand, we are pressed toward decisions that are not rational, in ordinary terms, but correspond, rather, to demands that would ordinarily be regarded as extravagant. In this duality, in this strange tension, lies the essence of ethics. The fear that an ethic based on reason would be something focused too low, would be too detached and heartless, is unfounded. When reason truly plumbs the depths of questions, it ceases to be cool reason and begins willy-nilly to speak with the melodies of the heart. And the heart, when it seeks to fathom itself, discovers that its realm reaches over into that of reason and that it must go through the land of reason in order to get to the further reaches of its own territory. How can that be?

Let's then explore the basic notion of goodness, first from the point of view of the heart and then from that of reason, and see if they converge.

The *heart* says that ethics is based on love. Let's examine that word "love." Love means harmony of being, community of being. Originally it applied to groups of persons who belonged to each other in some fashion so that they stood in some inner, reciprocal connection with each other: children and parents, married couples, and intimate friends. But now ethics requires that even people whom we do not know should not be regarded as strangers. The same applies to those who are worse than strangers to us because we have an aversion to them or because they have shown hostility toward us. We are, however, to treat them as if they were close to us. In the final analysis, then, the commandment of love means this: For you there are no strangers, only people whose well-being must be your concern. We often assume it to be natural to be concerned for those who are close to us and to be indifferent to those who are not. This natural disposition is not, however, permitted by ethical standards. And Jesus eliminated our behaving toward one another as strangers altogether when he said: The other person must mean as much to you as you do to yourself. You must feel what concerns him as that which concerns you directly.

The heart should explain the first commandment: "You should love God with all your heart and with all your mind and with all your strength." To love God, that remote, unfathomable being! Here it indeed becomes clear that the word "love," when it is used ethically, is used in a figurative sense. We ought to love God, who needs nothing from us, as if he were a creature we confront in daily life. In a human context, love means sharing experiences, having compassion, and helping each other. Toward God, however, love means something akin to reverential love. God is everlasting life. Thus, the most elementary principle, when grasped by the heart, means that out of reverence for the incomprehensible, infinite, and living One whom we call God, we should never consider ourselves strangers toward any person, rather, we are to coerce ourselves into being helpful to him and to share his experiences.

This, then, is what the heart says when it tries to give the most general meaning to the commandment of love for God and neighbor.

Now let *reason* speak. Let's assume that nothing about ethics has passed down to us and see how far we can get by pondering the forces that influence our actions. Will reason also make us step outside ourselves?

One usually hears it said that the only thing confirmed in reason is egotism. How can I make things good for myself? That is reason's wisdom, nothing more. At best, it can teach us a certain decency and justice, because these more or less belong to the feeling of happiness. Reason is the desire for knowledge and the desire for happiness, and both are mysteriously connected to each other in an inner way.

Desire for knowledge! You may seek to explore everything around you, you may push to the farthest limits of human knowledge, but in the end you will always strike upon something that is unfathomable. It is called life. And this mystery is so inexplicable that it renders the difference between knowledge and ignorance completely relative.

What difference is there between the scholar who observes the smallest and least expected signs of life under a microscope and the old peasant, who can scarcely read and write, when he stands in his garden in the spring and contemplates the blossoms bursting open on the branches of his tree? Both are confronted with the riddle of life! The one can describe it more thoroughly than the other, but for both it is equally inscrutable. All knowledge is finally knowledge of life. All realization is astonishment at this riddle of life—*reverence for life* in its infinite, yet ever new, manifestations. For what does it mean for something to come into being, live, and pass away? How amazing that it renews itself in other existences, passes away again, comes into being once more, and so on and so forth, from infinity to infinity? We can do all things and we can do nothing, for in all our wisdom we are not able to create life. Rather, what we create is dead!

Life means strength, will coming from the abyss and sinking into it again. Life means feeling, sensitivity, suffering. And if you are absorbed in life, if you see with perceptive eyes into this enormous animated chaos of creation, it suddenly seizes you with vertigo. In everything you recognize yourself again. The beetle that lies dead in your path—it was something that lived, that struggled for its existence like you, that rejoiced in the sun like you, that knew anxiety and pain like you. And now it is nothing more than decomposing material—as you, too, shall be sooner or later.

You walk outside and it is snowing. Carelessly you shake the snow from your sleeves. It attracts your attention: a snowflake glistens on your hand. You cannot help looking at it, whether you wish to or not. It glistens in its wonderful design; then it quivers, and the delicate needles of which it consists contract. It is no more; it has melted, dead in your hand. The flake, which fell upon your hand from infinite space, which glistened there, quivered, and died—that is you. Wherever you see life— that is you!

What is this recognition, this knowledge apprehended by the most learned and the most childlike alike? It is reverence for life, reverence for the impenetrable mystery that meets us in our universe, an existence different from ourselves in external appearance, yet inwardly of the same character with us, terribly similar, awesomely related. *The dissimilarity, the strangeness, between us and other creatures is here removed.*

Reverence before the infinity of life means the removal of the strangeness, the restoration of shared experiences and of compassion and sympathy. And thus the final result of knowledge is the same, in principle, as that which the commandment to love requires of us. Heart and reason agree together when we desire and dare to be men who attempt to fathom the depths of things.

And reason discovers the connecting link between love for God and love for man: love for all creatures, reverence for all being, a compassionate sharing of experiences with all of life, no matter how externally dissimilar to our own.

I can do no other than be reverent before everything that is called life. I can do no other than to have compassion for all that is called life. That is the beginning and the foundation of all ethics. Once one has experienced this and continues to experience it—and whoever experiences it once always continues to experience it!—he is ethical. He bears his morality in him and can never lose it, and it continues to develop in him. Whoever has not experienced it has only a superficially acquired morality. His ethical theories are not grounded in him, do not belong to him, and can drop away. And the terrible thing is that our entire generation possesses only such a superficially acquired ethic. When the time came for our ethic to be tested, it fell away from us. For centuries the human race has been trained with only a superficial ethic. We were brutal, ignorant, and heartless without suspecting it, because we did not yet have an adequate standard of value. We possessed no reverence for life.

You ought to *share life* and *preserve life*—that is the greatest commandment in its most elementary form. Another, and negative, way of expressing it is this: You shall *not kill*. We take this prohibition so lightly, thoughtlessly breaking flowers, thoughtlessly treading on the poor insect, and then—in terrible self-delusion, since everything avenges itself!—we thoughtlessly disregard the suffering and the lives of men and offer them to trivial earthly goals.

Much is said in our time about building a new humanity. How are we to build a new humanity? Only by leading men to a true, proper, inalienable ethic that is capable of development. But it will not succeed unless many individuals transform themselves from blind into seeing people and begin to spell out this great commandment, which says: reverence for life. More hangs on this than on the law and the prophets. It is the whole ethic of love in its deepest and in its highest sense. And it is the source of renewal again and again for the individual and for mankind.

2. SECOND SERMON ON REVERENCE FOR LIFE

None of us lives to himself, and none of us dies to himself.

ROM. 14:7, RSV

As I suggested last Sunday, we shall be concerned in our next meditations with the problems of ethics.

When the scribe posed the question about the greatest commandment of the Old Testament, Jesus replied by combining two commandments, that of love for God and that of love for one's neighbor. These then raised for us the question of the nature of ethics, of the ultimate, fundamental principle of morality. We were not content to accept the answer that the essence of ethics consists in love. Rather, we went on to ask: What really is love? What is love for God that impels us to be good to others? What is love for our neighbor? And we asked not only the heart but also the reason to explain the ethical—first, because we see that the weakness of our times lies in the lack of a morality based on reason, immune to prejudice and passion, and, second, because we cannot simply accept the fact that reason and heart can go together so effortlessly. The true heart is rational, and the true reason is sensitive. We discovered that both heart and reason agree that the good consists finally in the elemen-

13

tary reverence for the enigma we call life, in reverence for all of its manifestations, for the least as well as for the greatest of them. "Good" means to sustain and to advance life. "Evil" means to inhibit and to destroy life. We are ethical if we abandon our stubbornness, if we surrender our estrangement toward other creatures, and share in and empathize with that from their experience which surrounds us. Only in this capacity can we first truly become human. Only then do we possess an inalienable, continuously developing, and self-orienting ethic of our own.

The general expressions "reverence for life," "surrender of estrangement," "the urge to preserve life about us" all sound cold and empty. But even if they are insignificant words, they can nevertheless be rich in meaning. A seed is also insignificant, but it, too, bears within itself the structure of what grows out of it. Likewise, these simple words contain the basic attitude from which all morality develops, whether or not the individual is aware of it. Thus, the presupposition of morality is that we all share in everything that goes on around us, and that not only in human life but also in the life of all creatures. This recognition forces us all to do everything within our power for the preservation and advancement of life.

The great enemy of morality is indifference. As children, insofar as our understanding for such things went, we had an elementary capacity for compassion. But this ability did not grow through the years commensurately with our increasing understanding. It was something uncomfortable and embarrassing to us. We saw so many people who no longer possessed it. Then we, too, repressed sensitivity in order to be like the others, in order not to be different from them, and because we did not know any better. Thus, many people become like buildings in which one shop after another closes and which then look out cold and alien onto the street.

To remain good means to remain wide awake! We are all like a person walking outside in the cold and snow. Woe to him if he gives in to exhaustion, sits down, and sleeps; he will never awaken again. Similarly, the ethical person in us perishes if we grow weary of being compassionate with what others around us experience. Woe to us if our sensitivity is dulled; our true conscience in the broadest sense—that is, our consciousness of what we ought to do—is thereby ruined.

Reverence for life and sharing the life of others are what is important for our world. *Nature knows no reverence for life.* It produces life in thousands of the most meaningful ways and destroys it in thousands of the most senseless ways. At every stage of life up to the level of humanity, a terrible ignorance is poured out over creatures. They have only the will to live, but no capacity to share in what happens to others. They suffer, but they cannot have compassion. The great will to survive, by which nature is preserved, is *in puzzling self-contradiction* with itself. Creatures live at the cost of the lives of other creatures. Nature allows them to commit the most terrible cruelties. It leads insects instinctively to bore holes into other insects with their ovipositors and to lay their eggs in them so that their young may live from the caterpillar and torture it to death. Nature leads ants to band together and to attack a small creature and hound it to death. Look at the spider! How gruesome is the craft nature taught it!

Nature is beautiful and sublime, viewed from the outside. But to read in its book is horrible. And its cruelty is so senseless! The most precious life is sacrificed to the

15

most ignoble. A child breathes in the tuberculosis bacillus. He grows and thrives, but suffering and a premature death will be his lot because these lowly creatures multiply in his vital organs. How often in Africa I was horrified when I examined the blood of a man with sleeping sickness. Why did this man, his face contorted with pain, have to sit before me groaning, "Oh, my head, my head!"? Why should he have to cry night after night through and finally die miserably? Because there, under the microscope, minute pale corpuscles, ten- to fourteen-thousandths millimeters long, were present— oh, not very many, often only very few, so that one had to devote hours searching in order to discover even one!

This is thus the enigmatic rupture in the will to live—life against life, causing suffering and death, innocent and nevertheless guilty. Nature teaches cruel egoism, interrupted only for a short time by the urge it has placed in creatures to offer love and help to their young for as long as needed. But that the animal loves its own young with self-sacrifice even to the death, and thus can empathize in that instance, makes it only more horrible that it is denied sympathy for creatures unrelated to itself.

The world, delivered up to ignorant egoism, is like a valley that lies enshrouded in darkness. Only on the peaks above is there light. All must live in the darkness. One creature alone may ascend to see the light: the highest creature, *man.* He may achieve knowledge of reverence for life; he may aspire to knowledge of sharing and of compassion; he may step out and transcend the ignorance in which the rest of creation languishes.

And this understanding is the great event in the development of life. Here truth and goodness appear in the world. Light shines above the darkness. The most profound form of life is attained, life that is at the same time sharing the life of others. Here, in one existence, the breaking of the waves of the whole world is felt. Here, in one existence, life as such comes to consciousness of itself. Isolated individual existence ceases. Outside existence floods into ours.

We live in the world, and the world lives in us. But enigmas pile up around precisely this knowledge. Why do the law of nature and the ethical law diverge so sharply? Why can our reason not simply take over and develop what it discovers as expressions of life in nature? Why must reason come into such opposition to everything it sees? Why must it discover in itself laws completely different from those that rule the world? Why must it be on bad terms with the world just where it reaches the principle of goodness? Why must we experience this conflict without hope of ever being able to settle it? Why strife instead of harmony?

Furthermore, God is the power that sustains all. Why is the God who reveals himself in nature the negation of all that we experience as ethical? Why does a power at once create life rationally and destroy it irrationally? How do we reconcile God-the-power-of-nature with God-the-ethical-will, the God of love, as we must present him to ourselves when we have risen to a higher level of life, to reverence for life, to sharing and to compassion?

Several Sundays ago, while we were trying to clarify optimistic and pessimistic views of life, I told you that it is a great misfortune for our humanity that we cannot offer a harmonious philosophy of life. The more knowledge increases, the more it denies us such a view. And that is not only because it becomes ever clearer how little we really can grasp in knowledge but also because this contradiction within life itself becomes increasingly evident. *Our knowledge is in part,* says the Apostle Paul. That says far too little. It is still more difficult that our knowledge means insight into *unsolvable contradictions* . . . , all of which trace back to the one contradiction, namely, that the law according to which things take place has in itself nothing we can recognize and feel to be ethical.

Instead of being able to secure our morality in a consistent world view and in a unified concept of God, we must constantly protect it against the contradictions arising from the world view that, like a destructive surf, surges against it. We must build a dike against them. But will it hold?

The other thing that threatens our ability and will to empathize is the constantly recurring consideration: It is of no use! What you do and can do to prevent suffering, to alleviate suffering, to sustain life, are nothing in comparison with what happens in the world around you. And you are unable to do anything about it. Certainly it is terrible to be reminded of our helplessness. More still, of how much suffering we ourselves cause other creatures without our being able to prevent it.

You walk along a woodland path. The sun shines in bright patterns through the canopy. The birds sing. A thousand insects drone in the air. But your trail, unobtrusively as you pass, is death. Here you stepped on an ant and left it in pain. There is a little beetle that you squashed. Over there a worm, over which your foot has trodden, writhes in agony. Into the beautiful song of life, you, the innocent-guilty one, have introduced a melody of pain and death. And so, despite your wanting to do

God's will, you are conscious of a terrible powerlessness to help as you would like to. Then comes the voice of the tempter, saying to you, "Why torment yourself, then? It doesn't help. Give it up. Become unconcerned. Become thoughtless and uncaring like everyone else."

Still another temptation crops up. Compassion really involves the compassionate one in suffering. Once one has experienced the suffering of the world in himself, he can never again feel the superficial happiness that mankind desires. In hours that bring contentment and joy, one who is compassionate is unable to give himself unreservedly to their enjoyment, for the pain that he has co-suffered is there with him. What he has seen remains always with him. He thinks of the poor whom he has met, of the sick whom he has seen, of the people of whose difficult fate he has read, and darkness falls across the light of his joy. And so on and on.

In cheerful company such a person suddenly becomes absentminded. And then the tempter speaks again: "You cannot live like this. You must be able to detach yourself from what takes place around you. Don't be so supersensitive. Learn the necessary indifference. Put on your armor. Become thoughtless like everyone else if you want to live intelligently." In the end we go so far as to be ashamed to know the great experience of compassion and empathy. We hide it from each other and pretend it is something foolish, something that one lays aside when we begin to become mature and intelligent people.

These temptations unobtrusively ruin the presupposition of all goodness. Be watchful against them.

Counter the first by saying to yourself that compassion and lending assistance are an inner necessity for you. The utmost that you can do will always be, in view of what ought to be done, only a drop instead of a stream, but it gives to your life the only meaning it can have and that makes it valuable. Wherever you are, you should strive to bring redemption, redemption from the misery that the self-contradictory will has brought into the world, deliverance as only the person with understanding can bring it. Actually, the little you can do is considerable if it only relieves pain and suffering and anxiety from one creature, whether a person or some other creature. Preservation of life is the only true joy.

As for the other temptation, the fear that compassion toward what goes on around you will mean suffering for you, counter it by recognizing that sharing sorrow simultaneously gives you the capacity to share in joy. When you lack compassion, you lose simultaneously the capacity to share the happiness of others. And however little happiness we see in the world about us, sharing it, together with the good we produce, creates the only happiness that makes life bearable for us.

And finally you have absolutely no right to say, "I want to be so and so," because you think one way will make you happier than another. Rather, you must be as you must be: a true, knowing person, one who identifies with the world, one who experiences the world in himself. Whether you are happier or not on ordinary standards is a matter of indifference. The secret voice in us does not require happiness—to obey it is the only thing that can satisfy deeply.

So I say to you: Don't become indifferent. Remain alert! It is a matter of your souls! If I—and here in these words I expose my innermost thoughts!—were only able to force those of you who are here to destroy the deception with which the world wants to put us to sleep! If only you could cease to be thoughtless, that you could flinch no more before reverence for life and the necessity of learning reverence for life and true compassion. If only you could be absorbed into it. Then I should be satisfied and should regard my activity as blessed, even if I knew that tomorrow preaching were to be forbidden me or that my preaching to date had accomplished nothing more and from henceforth could accomplish nothing more.

Ordinarily, I shrink from influencing people because of the responsibility it entails, but I wish I now possessed the power to transform you, and make you sympathetic, until each of you experienced the great suffering from which one can never get free and gained the wisdom that comes of compassion. For then I should be able to tell myself that you were on the way to real goodness and could never again lose that. *None of us lives to himself!* May this word pursue us and not let us rest until we are laid in our graves!

3.

The righteous man cares for his beast; but a wicked man is cruel at heart.

PROV. 12:10, NEB

Reverence for life, as we saw in our previous two meditations, is the fundamental law of ethics. Sharing and being compassionate with that which the living creatures about us suffer. From this fundamental belief alone comes the act that is able everywhere to confirm man as ethical. But the great danger here is that we may become weary in this true humanity. Indeed, such weariness has three causes.

In the first place, this ethical law concerning true humanity is incapable of creating an appropriate, unified worldview. We see, on the one hand, how in nature everything inclines more to egoism and cruelty than to a divinely willed law. On the other hand, we feel that in reverence for life we are drawing near true knowledge and understanding. The God of love who meets us in love cannot be united with the God who encounters us in nature. The ethical law cannot be made consonant with the laws of nature.

A second cause of our weariness lies in the fact that compassion means suffering. Whoever is open to all of the pain occurring around him can no longer be happy

22

and unembarrassed. Then the tempter speaks and says, "One cannot live like this. Be apathetic like the others!"

The third cause is the doubt that grips us when we see just how small what we do to help really is, especially in comparison with what is going on, without our being able to prevent it. Here, then, the tempter says, "It's no use. Don't torment yourself. Become like the others!"

So if we do not remain watchful, we grow weary and lose the inner drive for ethics. We must understand that we have to live that way, that true humanity is the only happiness. It is our great mysterious duty in the world.

And now we want to consider together *the practical questions of morality.* Today we begin with the question of our *conduct toward living creatures.*

I have already told you that I demand something much more general than compassion toward animals. It must grow from the ground of a general reverence for everything that life is. Otherwise it is incomplete and inconstant. The history of compassion toward animals shows that clearly.

The ancient pagans already knew compassion toward animals. In Athens, according to one account, a boy was condemned to death because he had torn out the eyes of a crow. That horses and other draft animals were put out to pasture in their old age is reported many times.

In the Old Testament animals are often thought of with affection. Thus, the commandment about the Sabbath mandated that animals, too, should have rest on feast days. It is expressly forbidden that the ox who stamps out the grain on the threshing floor should have his mouth bound. Later, the Apostle Paul, in a marvelous passage in his letter to the Romans, describes how even the creatures sigh with us to be freed from anxiety and perishability.

Albert Schweitzer

But, nevertheless, Christianity did not follow any further the ethical demands that ought to determine our behavior toward living creatures. Throughout the centuries one finds the greatest thoughtlessness and crudeness bound together with the most earnest piety. One thinks less about what we ought to be toward the poor creatures than again and again about how one can make the most of the difference between man and them. Man should not experience the inner-relatedness that exists among all living things, we say, but, rather, ought always to prompt himself: "You have an immortal soul. The animal does not. An unbridgeable chasm lies between us," . . . as if we really knew something about it.

Thus, Christianity, from the first centuries up until deep in the Middle Ages, did not ennoble people in their behavior toward living creatures, did not make them into people who understood. Only with awakening thought does there appear consideration of what sins we have committed against the poor creatures.

It was Martin Luther in the first instance who, in almost fainthearted fashion, admitted it. His servant had fashioned a bird net in order to catch migrating birds. In response, and in order to dissuade him from his goal, Luther prepared a humorous petition from the birds to the servant so that he might be able to forbid him this evil craft.

The Alsatian [Philipp Jakob] Spener went much further in the declining years of the seventeenth century. In his catechism, he dared expressly to teach that, according to its spirit, the commandment "Thou shalt not kill" contained within itself the prohibition against unnecessarily killing or torturing animals.

The hymnal of the church at Mühlhausen in Alsace from the year 1826 even contains a hymn about compassion for animals.

Today's movement for the prevention of cruelty to animals goes back to the Stuttgart pastor Christian Adam Dann, who was the first to provide an extended presentation of our duties toward animals. He was impelled to the task when he had to witness a cruel man kill a stork. Then and there he formed the resolution to write down everything he saw of mistreatment of animals and thereby to shock his readers. His book appeared at the beginning of the nineteenth century at the time of the Napoleonic Wars. At the end of his book, he apologized that he drew people's attention to animals when so many people were bleeding and suffering. But, he said, if men have brought it upon themselves mutually to kill each other, then that is because they have not been trained in compassion from their youth on and have even fallen into maltreatment of living creatures. Therefore, the call to *compassion with the animals*, even in a time when our pain costs grief to many people, is *not untimely.*

The movement to prevent cruelty to animals has not gone to sleep again since that time. But it has not awakened the conscience of our humanity. Our true relationship to living creatures has not become obvious to us, because that general principle belongs there— reverence for life as such, the great sharing—as the great understanding of life. Everything else remains imperfect and is built on sand.

How far down does the boundary of conscious, feeling life reach? No one can say. Where does the animal stop and the plant begin? And the plants: Is it possible that they feel and are sensitive even if we cannot demonstrate it? Is not every life process, right down to the uniting of two elements, bound up with something like feeling and sensitivity?

25

Then every being must be holy to us. We may not destroy anything of it carelessly. Tear off no flower, no leaf! If you see a little plant, even one of the most ordinary sort, in front of you on your pathway, walk so as not to step on it if you can possibly avoid it. If you are walking with children in the out-of-doors, do not let them thoughtlessly pluck flowers. In the first hour they wilt in the children's hot little hands and are thrown away thoughtlessly because they then become inconvenient to them. Rather, dare to teach them reverence for life from their first years onward. Even make yourselves look ridiculous in front of thoughtless people who make fun of such fads, for all I care. But the children will be grasped by the awe of the mystery and will thank you sometime that you awakened in them the great melody of reverence for life. The hecklers themselves will also be more moved than they would like to admit by the elementary truth in that which touches them in such unfamiliar ways.

But precisely here the difficulty that is given in nature through its *self-division of the will to live* emerges. Man cannot take his nourishment from the air and the earth as the plants do. He needs the plants in order to be able to live. The higher form of life destroys the lower in order to live from it. Mercilessly our scythes go through the meadows at the time when the flowers all bloom and cut them down dead because we need them as food for our domestic animals. When necessity leads us, we arrogate to ourselves the right to wreak massive destruction, and we can do no other. But precisely because we do stand so clearly under the terrible law of nature, which permits living beings to kill other living beings, we must watch with anxiety that we *do not destroy out of thoughtlessness*, where we do not stand under any pressure of necessity. We must perceive every act of destruction always as something terrible and ask ourselves, in every single case, whether we can bear the responsibility as to whether it is necessary or not.

Indeed, what a terrible thoughtlessness it is, morally considered, to decorate rooms with cut flowers and to rejoice in cut flowers, perhaps even wound on wire. The sight is beautiful, certainly. We bring nature into the room. But nature in what condition? Dying nature! The flowers in the vase die prematurely in order to please you. The picture over which you rejoice is the picture of death! I know how exaggerated all of this must sound to our hereditary thoughtlessness. But whoever begins to reflect a bit concerning what we do is not free to stop wherever he chooses. He must, rather, always be led back to reverence for life as to the highest law that stands over all customs and is appointed to rule everything. One day the time will come when all children will read in schoolbooks up to which century people in naive cruelty pleased themselves with dying flowers.

Directed toward animals, reverence for life means, first, that *killing animals may be neither drama nor sport!*

Not drama: I can still see myself on a radiant autumn Sunday in the great plaza of Barcelona. In bright dresses and fluttering head scarves, women and girls were all going in one direction: to the arena! They were going in order to witness how enraged bulls slit open the bellies of poor mules with their horns—and then how they themselves, to the jubilation of the crowd, were finally tortured to death. The director of the large music society whose guest I was addressed me, saying, "You must come! You must have seen it at least once; otherwise you won't know what Spain is! All of the other musicians have always come along." The man was a deeply pious artist with whom I had been conversing just that morning so seriously concerning Christianity. He did not understand why I could never have forgiven myself had I gone with him, and left me on my own in order to be sure not to miss the start. And you know, arenas for bullfights have been built in southern Europe again during the last two centuries, whereas they were earlier forbidden. In another century perhaps they will be found all over Europe.

And hunting? Is that to be condemned as well? Hunting as the necessary killing of all sorts of beasts of the field, whether for food or to defend against their overpopulating the area, is not condemned. But hunting as an amusement: yes! Hunting may be a necessary craft, like that of the slaughterer, in which a gun is used instead of working with an ax and a knife. But not as an amusement. That for so long it has passed as an amusement, even as a sort of training ground for manhood, will someday be cited as one of the most meaningful facts in the history of the spiritual life. And those who think that such sensitivity causes the species to grow soft cannot be allowed to disconcert us. Manliness that shows itself in thoughtless joy in destruction and torture is not authentic manliness.

For myself, that all became clear to me as a child, especially in one noteworthy experience. The neighbor's boy and I had made slingshots. One Sunday morning (it was Lent) he said to me, "Come on. Let's go into the garden in front of the church behind the village and get some sparrows from the trees with our slings!" The idea made me uncomfortable. It was appropriate neither to

Sunday nor to spring, and I feared in advance seeing the birds that were to be killed by us—but I didn't dare to make myself appear ridiculous. In front of a leafless tree on which the birds were chirping, we stopped cautiously and, with serious looks on our faces, set up our slings. Then all at once the bell rang softly from the tower into the still spring day. A terrible grief came over me, as if voices were calling to us not to commit that great sin. I broke away and dashed home and knew (I was, I believe, in my first year of school at the time) that I had experienced something decisive for my whole life. I have more fear of the memory of that bell than of being ridiculous, when, ever since that time, I dare not to be afraid of others in representing convictions that in terms of contemporary views appear exaggerated—even though they are only truisms.

In the presence of a particular temptation to neglect reverence for life, we must all protect ourselves: We easily become compassionless toward the unpleasant creature or toward that which we know as evil. If we see a toad, for instance, we seem to have an instinct to throw a stone at it. And to exterminate rats, mice, and other rodents, we seem to think any means is acceptable, even that which we know will produce terribly long torment and mortal agony in the animal. We must free ourselves of that. Even toward the unpleasant and pernicious animal we must always, in every single case, remain conscious of our responsibility. Only when it is a necessity may we kill it, and even then we must consider how to do this with the least painful means. We may not become cruel either from fear or from repugnance.

A special question: In the battle of life against life that plays itself out in nature, may I choose sides? May I involve myself in it? For instance, out there on the ground crawls a large spider. I know that she will capture many insects in the web she will spin. She will torture and kill them. One step from me squashes her and removes much pain for many from the world. May I do that? Should I do that? Here no universally valid decision can be given. Rather, you must deal with every individual case according to your conviction and to your conscience. Perhaps one time you will do one thing and another time another.

Around my house in Africa stand palm trees from which the nests of the weaverbird hang down. When the young birds came out, large hawks appeared and ate them amid the grieving shrieks of the older birds. This sorrow gave me the right to slay the robbers. But when we passed by a sandbank on which an alligator was sleeping, I did not shoot at him (as the others usually did—they did it for sport). That was the case even though I could imagine just what sort of devastation he would wreak at night among the fish. But I did not catch him in the act and did not want to take the guilt on myself should he, wounded, dive into the water and suffer there.

These decisions can go either way. If only you act responsibly and according to conscience, and not thoughtlessly, you are justified.

Becoming conscious of our responsibility also means that we *do everything in order to prevent suffering* when something happens to an animal where we can have influence. For many people, suffering does not exist if they do not need to witness it. They flee and never consider that, precisely by this inability to see, they become guilty. The housewife cannot stand to be present to see how the fish or the chicken is killed, so she runs out, slams the door, and puts her hands in front of her face. She gives the job over to the servant girl, to whom it is equally unpleasant. Then, because she must do the deed, the servant, in her hopeless inexperience, uses the worst possible methods. Afterward the housewife returns and is relieved that "everything is ready." But in the tortured face of the dead animal she can read the truth—that she omitted the last service of love we owed it.

Therefore, do not train your children to hide like that. They must know how one best accomplishes the killing that accompanies ordinary life, and they must teach and supervise those who do it. In Africa, where one must do all of his own slaughtering, I force myself whenever possible to be present in order to prevent all unnecessary pain to the animal. If cats must be done away with, do not try to drown them and think that everything is well when they are out of sight. They may survive for hours in misery in the water. Instead, kill them yourself with a hammer blow to the head. That is your duty toward them.

That we are forced variously to destroy life, whether for our sustenance, with respect to animals that are born and that we cannot sustain and that must be done away with, or in order to protect ourselves from dangerous animals—that is the terrible law of the division of the will to life to which we are subject. But we are never permitted to give ourselves over to it thoughtlessly. It is for us always equally terrible, equally uncomfortable. But the one thing we can and must do is this. We must consider our responsibility in every individual case, we must test the necessity, and then we must proceed in the most considerate way possible.

Has a horse served a well-to-do farmer faithfully?

Then the farmer has no right when, thanks to its age, it becomes unable to serve him further to sell it into hands that will torture it in order to wrest from it every last ounce of service. Rather, he should either allow it to be put out to pasture or sell it for slaughter.

But we should *not only not kill; we should sustain life* where that is possible. That we are subject in a thousandfold ways to the law, that in order to live we must offer the lower form of life to the higher, is terrible. There is only one thing that, with time, allows us to forget and transposes us into another world: sustaining life and the ability to help. Keep your eyes open so that you do not miss any opportunity where you can be a redeemer! Do not go carelessly past the poor insect that has fallen into the water, for instance, but imagine what it means to struggle with a watery death. Help it to get out with a hook or a piece of wood. Then, when it cleans its wings, you know you have experienced something wonderful: the happiness of having saved life, of having acted on behalf of and in the fullness of the power of God. The worm on the hard street, onto which he has strayed by error, languishes because he cannot bore into it. Put him on soft earth or in the grass! "What you have done to one of the least of these, you have done to me." This word of Jesus is valid for us all, and it ought to determine what we do also to the least among living creatures.

Whoever does not know the heights we then experience, when the wonderful light of being able to help falls into the gruesome night of having to destroy, does not know how rich life can be.

And here, too: *Do not worry about the usual prejudices.* Do not be afraid to be ridiculous. *But act!* What you are doing belongs to part of what it means to be a human being. Where you yourself see it in others, does it not strike you as if the act reconciled you and the person and life, with which you have been internally at odds? On a dark winter's evening, when the horses cannot pull the heavy wagon up the arch of the bridge because of the ice and snow and a few passersby lend their hands and push, is it not so for you? However small the helping act, when you encounter it, it is as if the dark winter's evening is absorbed, and you proceed on in a wonderful night! And are these men with whom you laid your hands to the wagon then not closer to you through this insignificant, natural act than many others with whom you have discussed so many things?

4.

Judge not, that you be not judged.

MATT. 7:1, RSV

Reverence for the life of the lower creatures occupied us in our last meditation. We sought to understand to what degree we have the right to offer the lower being to the higher and what duty we have, whenever we are able to do it, to prevent suffering and death for all living creatures. In every moment, I said, we must be conscious of our responsibility for what we undertake with the living creature or what we subject it to. We must also free ourselves from the thoughtlessness with which the ordinary person sins against a living creature. At the same time, we must consider the fact that we modern people owe a great debt of gratitude to these creatures. The means with which sicknesses can be healed and pains stilled, we owe in large measure to the poor creatures who had to be given over to the tests that brought medicine forward. Whatever good we do to an animal is thus always only a payment on a debt of thanks we owe it for what the suffering creature has won for us.

And now: *What does reverence for human life mean?* What does this reverence enjoin upon me? What does my sharing the experiences of the life of people around me enjoin upon me?

Reverence for the life of man begins with *reverence for one's own existence*. Man, the philosopher Hegel once said, as the highest being, has the great freedom, that he can set a goal for his life. That we continue to live is an ethical act. For many people it is an unconscious act. It is made easier for them and is urged on them by a horror in the presence of the great unknown called death. And it comes to them through a comforting thoughtlessness in terms of which that little bit of pleasure life can offer makes it to appear to them worth living for. Whoever dares to think, however, whoever poses questions to existence, whoever tries to understand the meaning of the existence he bears, whoever shares the pain of the world, knows hours in which the horror of existence is greater than the horror of no longer existing. Even if he appears to others as a happy person, perhaps even as a jovial person, the temptation comes to him somehow to put an end to his life. You walk alongside people and think you know them, but you don't, because you do not know that they have lived through such hours where they vacillated over whether to decide for existence or for nonexistence. Have you never stood at a grave—the shrubbery played in the autumnal wind or the spring flowers moved in the breezes—and in the silence of the cemetery the world foundered, your existence foundered, and a terrible longing to rest then encompassed you also, . . . and you, as in pain, came to again and departed?

Thus, for everyone who truly gets acquainted with life, there comes a crisis in which this existence becomes worthless to him, even though he still carries on with it. Only reverence for life can lead us out of that crisis: We live out of duty. There is a deeper sense in the idea that we must all be born again in order to be what God

requires of us. We must all be born again from the
unconscious will to life to the higher, conscious will in
which we then live. Because life in itself is so dark, it
remains so inexplicable, it appears to us as puzzlingly
precious. In the confused noise of the world, we hear the
eternal song of life like a pure, clear melody suspended
over the whole and allow ourselves by this means to
manage whatever our fate may be.

To reverence for our own existence comes
reverence for the life that takes its start from us. *What
right have we to bring other people into being?*
Look at your child in its cradle. What will its life be?
It will bear the same burden as you. Perhaps it will be
bodily or spiritually ruined. And you, you load on him
the burden of existence, you co-bear the responsibility
that the terrible game of human existence goes on from
generation to generation. It is said that Indian Buddhism
prepares itself in the world to end conquests. Whether it
comes to that or not, the world view it represents is a
great temptation. It teaches the redemption of the world
in the cessation of life. When there is no more humanity,
no one more will be born to sorrow and pain. Then
blessedness is poured out over the world.
One need not import this idea from without. It is
already in us. And we must come to terms with it and
overcome it with its opposite claim, that this is the
truth: that the most people possible experience life in the
world, that there is a world purpose that wants the most
people possible to experience existence, and that we bow
to it and regard every new human existence as something
valuable for the world, as something that ought to be.
The opposite idea, that of the diminution of the being of

man in the world, is seen as sin. For that notion, however, there is no foundation other than reverence for life. One cannot say that humanity realizes some sort of purpose in the world, but, rather, that it is itself purpose.

Even here we wander between puzzles: Reverence for the highest life orders us *not to take even the senseless or agonizing life of man.* If I see an animal that suffers, I may be his redeemer in that I put an end to his existence. With a suffering person, however, I may not do so. I ought not shorten his life by even an hour.

And I must bear my own existence even if it means only more pain and torment. In these cases one can still say that existence still makes sense in that we live before others with pain and suffering in a model fashion and purify ourselves in suffering. That is true even when, as in many cases, the torment is such that there can be no thought of a conscious reflection on and a spiritual assimilation of the pain. However, the puzzle confronts us in its whole horror when it is a matter of human beings in whom human reason is lacking and whom we sustain in existence solely out of reverence for human life in itself.

Several years ago an old physician told me of a temptation he had experienced. He was called to a feebleminded child who was sick with diphtheria. A few hours' delay in the administration of the appropriate treatment and the child would be freed from his suffering existence. "I fought with myself," he said, "and in the end, reverence for life triumphed. The child was saved, and I bear the responsibility that his miserable existence goes on from year to year."

We are not able to solve the puzzles that turn up

here. You have built for yourself the most attractive world view and go by the barred windows of a mental hospital. Look at the misery that lives behind them and you have to think thoughts about irremediable, senseless life. Everything you had thought goes to ruin. In the world view there is room only for the rational, developable personal existence, not for the irretrievably senseless.

Thus we enter through the door of reverence for our own existence into the area of morality and see, as if we were going over a bridge, into an abyss of insoluble problems. We want to leave them behind, and proceeding, we turn our gaze away in order to look forward, but they nevertheless force us to look back again and again.

Reverence for life, turned toward human existence, means not only reverence for being as such, as with living creatures, but *reverence for all values and purposes* that are given to this highest being. I can conceive of my life as worth living in the deeper sense only when I bring it to its highest value, that is, when I drive toward its spiritual and ethical fulfillment. And in reverence for the life of the other, this reverence for the destiny of human life is likewise given. What I understand as the urgent goal of life in us is this: that my life, together with the life of all people, may be brought to its highest value. That is the world idea as I experience it in myself.

In saying that, I have *not explained the world*. The purpose of nature, with her thousands of appearances of life, is not understood by that, for nature is not merely the presuppositions of man's existence. And when I lift my eyes to the sky and say to myself that these luminous points up there mean an infinity of worlds, then my existence and that of humanity become so small by comparison that I am unable to think of the fulfillment of this human being as the purpose of the world. Nature is not the presupposition of humanity, and humanity may not conceive of itself as the purpose of the infinite world, the infinity of worlds—yet nevertheless the fulfillment of man is the only purpose we can give to his existence in general. That is the difficulty that is constantly reappearing in every attempt to create a meaningful world view and that meets us in thousands of always-new forms in thought and in religion.

That the world should exist for the sake of paltry little humanity, where we appear to ourselves in the infinity of being as something infinitesimally small, almost accidental, is the offense we have already felt as children when our thought processes awoke. This only deepens the further we come. The idea that the perfection of the individual and of humanity is the only purpose that we can discover in existence and that we feel to be natural is not given so we can build a world-view with it. Rather, we are to instruct ourselves again and again to take it in itself and for itself, to hold fast to it as something we experience elementarily but cannot take further. Only in one thing are we able to guess at it: The development of man and of humanity fulfills and outstrips the existence of the huge world because it deals with something *spiritual*. And where the spiritual begins, the standards with which one can measure and compare things cease. In man and in humanity, God, the spirit of the worlds, comes, as the mystics always said, to consciousness of himself and indeed to an ever purer self-consciousness the more man and humanity spiritually and morally perfect themselves. This is the monstrous, mysterious, peculiar phenomenon in what happens, and to this extent, the perfection of man and of humanity can be understood as the end purpose of the world. But that is true only as in dreamlike guesses, for the enigmas that pile up against us here are not explained.

Morality is therefore that to me my own existence and the existence of every man is holy and that I am convinced of the higher destiny of my own being, as I am of that of every man, and that I act accordingly.

Negatively put, morality thus means that I join in nothing injurious to the existence of a person but, rather, that I leave untouched his possessions, his position, his happiness, his name, his reputation, and everything that belongs to his existence.

How far can we carry through on that? As far as our mind reaches, to begin with. What obstructs our minds? Thoughtlessness, envy, and hatred. With these three enemies, every one of us must fight his life long. Let's take the most visible first, hatred. I am not to injure a man in his existence in any way, even if he is unpleasant and odious to me and even if he has done me evil. We learn that from youth on, and we feel instinctively that that is true. Every time we commit a malicious act, even if we have many good reasons for it, and even if we want to make ourselves clear that we are acting not from personal but from objective motives, we hear a clear word within saying to us that we are about to blunder. Finally, we let ourselves become insensible to the situation and act according to the rules of "an eye for an eye, and a tooth for a tooth," fraud for fraud, suspicion for suspicion, slander for slander, such as we commonly see in daily life around us. With that we are on our way to spiritual ruin, for nothing gnaws away at our souls like that and so brings us down. And when we so sink into the night of the world, the wonderful words of the Lord glitter over us: "Love your enemies; bless those who persecute you; do good to those who hate you; pray for those who insult you and persecute you because you are children of your Father in heaven," as well as the saying of the Apostle: "If your enemy hungers, feed him; if he thirst, give him to drink; when you do that, you will heap fiery coals on his head."

How do these words go down with us? Let's be completely honest and admit that our minds contend against these things. None of us would consider wanting to annul these words, but we do picture to ourselves the situations in which we would want to follow them, and we are disposed to feel at the outset a certain self-satisfaction concerning our own magnanimity. Every one of us, when he comes upon a person who has sunk very low, pictures himself as one who would generously help if the person were in need, as one who would repay him good for evil. But these spectacular acts of love with which we amuse ourselves we find no opportunity to carry out. How lovely it would be to give our enemy—I mean our personal enemy—something to drink when he languishes or to feed him when he is hungry—but look: He doesn't need us at all, for he has enough to eat and drink. Nor in any other way does he come into a position so that we can, to his shame, correctly show what Christian love of one's enemy is. If we want in some other way to show him that we love him and to heap fiery coals on his head, he won't permit it and misunderstands and ridicules us in every way. Even our apology is something he does not want. In short, our enemies will not cooperate with our needs for magnanimous gestures toward them. And because our enemies do not conform to the noble mind that we imagine we bear in ourselves, we feel ourselves misunderstood, disappointed, and finally act like the average person around us. And why is that? Because our minds have not come to terms with reality.

Who in us is deceived by the world concerning our noble mind? Not the true person in us but the actor. In each of us there lives an actor who accompanies us throughout our lives and who longs for good roles to play. And we exchange ethics for the good roles we intend for him to play. The loveliest role, that which he likes to play best, is magnanimity. And because he cannot play it, he says to the person in us, "Life doesn't allow us to be ethical." So long as the dreamer, the fantasizer— precisely this actor who wants to bask in the role of magnanimity—still has input into your ethics and wants to find satisfaction in it, you will bring it to nothing. Be wary of wanting to appear magnanimous before men; beware of appearing magnanimous to yourself. Abandon everything in your ideas that somehow has to do with magnanimity as one would knock down a crooked old corner of a city in order to put in broad streets into which the sun shines and to build houses in which one can live. The result is not so poetic or so artistic, but it is preferable.

So it is with your morality. Do not go after spectacular displays of love for your enemy—it is likely that in your whole life you won't experience one—but, rather, build from the bottom up. Do the insignificant and the hidden things that are much more difficult than the acknowledgedly grand gesture. Then you will do the grand gesture as it ought to be done and is done in the spirit of Jesus: unconsciously.

The simple deed, which is so difficult when you are on bad terms with a person, is to suppress an unfriendly word or a hateful allusion concerning him. This would be something, for instance, that you could lodge somewhere where no one knows how things are between you and him. Or when he irritates you somewhere, act as if you were unaware of it. Or when someone offers you something on him, have no interest in it. Where you could damage him, restrain yourself. Do not speak of that which he has done to you, even when you could put him in the wrong a hundred times before people. All of that belongs to the insignificant phrase "not to interfere in his existence in a damaging way" and is the preschool, the difficult preschool, of morality.

This morality does not submit to formulation into commandments, but, rather, it grows like a shrub in big and little impulses from reverence for the life of the other. For in the final analysis, nothing sustains you in this daily effort other than that again and again you refer back to the consideration: He is a person like me. What I know of him is not his whole existence. As I am in many things better than the people from whom something separates me want to suspect and to allow to be true, so, too, is he. And as I am worse, so terribly much worse than the honor in which I make my way in society and that is conceded to me in so many things, so, too, is he. As I, in the longing and pain I bear in myself and the ideals that reign in me, am a much different person from what I ever allow to be known, so, too, is he. None of us can say "I know so and so," even when he lives in the same house with him and shares his life. Rather, each person (and often the closer we are to him the truer this is) is finally for us a mystery. How good and evil, longing after ideals and being exhausted permeate his life and determine his decisions, and how the fate that controls him is formed remain unknown. And because his life is a puzzle to you, when you go deeply into these ideas, then you live in such reverence for all human existence that you no longer recognize the right that thoughtless people take in some sort of passion to interfere in his life. It is no longer the life of a personal enemy for you but life radically viewed—something you do not dare touch in order to disturb it, but only in order to build it up.

I dare to speak so terribly soberly and coolly because I have the certainty that precisely in the reverence for life lies something so great and overpowering that the enthusiasm that must bear us through life, if we are to serve the good, is given in it like a great, calm melody.

5.

But I say to you, do not resist evil . . .

MATT. 5:39a

*Lord, how often shall my brother sin
against me and I forgive him? As many as
seven times?*

MATT. 18:21b

Jesus' principle, that we may never interfere injuriously in the life of a person out of hate or
aversion even if admittedly he merits no sympathy and
has done us evil, is one we must therefore place at the
head of every morality. Upon our observance of it depends whether we remain moral or not. It is not only the
most intimate challenge of ethics; it is also that which is
subject to no limitation, which brings us into no conflict
with ourselves, and which depends for whether we fulfill
it solely on our own dispositions. With all the other
demands of ethics we shall meet, the ideal has to be set
over against reality and reality's demands be accommo-
dated. But with this one, I myself am master over this
immense area of daily morality that is fundamental to
reciprocal relations between people. Here you need not
worry if you are understood, for whether understood or
misunderstood, you can always follow the ideal.

With the next question that surfaces, the *opposition between ideal and reality* is directly engaged. It is the matter of how far I must yield to those who, in a *malicious* manner, injure my existence.

Our Lord Jesus has here set the ideal in his Sermon on the Mount, when he said: *"Do not resist evil, but if anyone strikes you on the right cheek, turn to him the other also; and if any man would sue you and take your coat, let him have your cloak as well; and if any man forces you to go one mile, go with him two"* (Matt. 5:39–41). The fundamental idea he lays down in these most extreme examples gives us some insight. We are not to defend against every injury to our existence immediately, but are, rather, to accustom ourselves to bear injustice patiently with calmness and indulgence. We are not to think that with every injustice that occurs to us our very existence is immediately threatened. Jesus himself turned against this instinctive reaction to everything that is done to us.

Let's understand it this way: You ought not prepare yourself to offer resistance immediately to every evil that meets you. You ought rather to train yourself in order that the slander, lies, intrigue, and injuries that come upon you are treated as something you put up with, as something that must come about. Work inwardly on yourself so that you come out above all of this. Learn the great forgiveness of disregard. Of the injustice that meets you, fifty percent lies in the circumstances, twenty-five percent in ignorance, and only twenty-five percent in genuine malevolence.

And *you yourself are also ensnared in doing equal injury* to the existence of *other* people. Consider what untested gossip you pass on, what slander one expresses against another person! Take away what the circumstances have to do with the injustice and the cruelty that confront you. Take away what people in their thoughtlessness do to damage you, just as you damage others. . . . What still remains for you to get furious about?

Peter asked the Lord—they were already on the way toward the Passion in Jerusalem—whether it was enough if he forgave his brother seven times. He answered him: "Not seven times, but seventy times seven times." He then added to that response the parable of the man who, because of his debt of ten thousand talents, faced his family's and all of his goods' being sold and his going to prison and then was released from all his debt. He goes on to say how this man, then, finds one of his fellow servants who owed him one hundred denarii, attacked him, seized him by the throat, and had him thrown into prison despite all of his pleas. This is so terribly true for us all, if we dare to look at our life as it really is.

Moreover, in much that encounters us, where outwardly we have the right to be angry and to resist because of an injustice, we do not have the right inwardly. Make yourself a secret account of what you have neglected in thoughtlessness or in meanness in consideration of some other person's existence. You will come to the recognition that you must atone for that, in that you have to allow similar things to happen to you. Be as wary of your anger as you must be of your magnanimity. Only he understands life who balances what he himself inflicts on others by that which he experiences. Thereby he has pressed through to the knowledge that we must see much that happens to us as atonement for that which our guilt represents to other people. He, then, is freed up from the superficial feeling of injustice that allows us to get defensive in a blind and rash fashion at all that injures us, things great and small. That is the deep meaning of the commandment of Jesus that we not resist evil.

Jesus expressed this absolutely: "That you should not resist evil at all." This he verified with drastic examples. How did he come to do that? Because he wants to awaken the mind in all of its elementary power, he therefore demands the absolute. Then, because he attributes to the world only a short continued existence and awaits a new heaven, a new earth, and a new mankind transfigured into a supernatural humanity for the next times, the opposition of this absolute demand to reality in this, as in so many other questions, is thereby suspended.

But we, we who have to reckon with the continuation of the course of the world and of our existence, we must allow ourselves to oppose that absolute demand with reality. And we must allow that a moment can come when we have the right to take up our defense against unjust injury to our existence. As an example, one can adduce Jesus himself, who, in spite of his word about the other cheek that one is to offer to him who has struck the first, did not act according to that principle when the officer struck him before the court—if John the Evangelist has correctly reported to us—but called him to account.

But where do right and duty of defense *begin*?

No one can settle that for you. You must determine that for yourself in every case. In general, we say that where our existence as such is threatened, whether through violence, through injustice, or through slander, we have the right and the duty to rebel. But the decision whether our existence is really threatened is a completely personal and conjectural one. Often slanders, which we are inclined to let alone, are much more dangerous to us, even among our acquaintances, than this or that apparently much more serious undertaking against us. We can, however, propose a general principle, namely, that we are all more likely to conclude too quickly that we are really threatened than we are to underestimate the threat. Let this reflection lead you and let yourself seriously test in every case whether a defense of some sort is necessary or whether you ought not rather take the word about not resisting evil as operative.

Not to interfere with the life of another injuriously out of hatred, to bear what one does to you without defense, and to be able to forgive everything—that is the foundation of the ethical personality. Whoever is not clear about himself and does not work on himself and against the banal and common that reigns in us in this respect, and whoever does not fight with deep, goal-conscious reflection, will not find the narrow gate of morality. In spite of all his better impulses, he will bring it to nothing, because the ground is not prepared.

I know a merchant. He is already very old. A generation ago he discovered that his partner, who handled the books, had for years swindled him and defrauded him of thousands. He could prove it sum for sum and might have committed him to prison and secured the restoration of a large sum. But as his partner pleaded with him for mercy for his children's sake, he let himself be moved. He did not require the sum of money back, and he also kept the other man on in the firm. His partner never thanked him for that, nor did his son, and the firm suffers still from the loss it sustained at that time. More than once it has been in danger of going under. And still the merchant's children do not think ill of their father for doing what he once did. They might have had a very different life had he, at that time, as was his right, made his claims against the swindler. But they know that this deed is a spiritual will that makes them and their children and their children's children inwardly rich.

But now the second great question: The maintaining of my existence brings me not only into the situation where I must defend against interference in it, but also where I injure the existence of others, with or without my being aware of it. In the older books on ethical teachings, there is always such a neat division between duties toward one's self and duties toward one's neighbor. In reality, however, we are unable to hold these apart as cleanly as we should like to. In the effort to practice legitimate self-preservation, I find myself forced to interfere injuriously in the life of others. The self-division of the will to life, as it appears in the human fight for one's existence, brings this with it. It is not always possible to harmonize my livelihood and that of every other person.

I am a merchant. My business goes well, and the numbers of my customers increase. I am happy about it. But what more I earn is another's loss, another who is perhaps just as conscientious and hardworking as I, only I am more skilled and have, perhaps, more capital.

Someone puts forward an improvement of a machine that reduces the production costs of a particular article by some percentage points. His patent brings him a lot of money, and he is praised as a great inventor. But his fortune is bought with the misfortune of many others who do not possess the capital to equip their firms with the improved machines, and they necessarily go to ruin.

I apply for a position and have excellent prospects of getting the job. Another person, who has it much more difficult than I and has set his last hopes on precisely this job, has to retire because I have been seen as the one better qualified for this position than he. May I allow this to happen? Can I bear the responsibility for the fact that because I stand in his way, he is damaged?

The world says, "What is not attained with bad means need give you no worry. You bear no responsibility. That's the way things go. What is one person's good fortune is another's misfortune." But however reasonable and correct that sounds to you, you may not rest with it yet. You may not say, "That is a law against which one can do nothing." Rather, you must feel the responsibility and decide in each case whether it is *really* necessary, for the sake of your getting on, that another should suffer this or that damage. We must all do battle against the inconsiderateness that life and society want to teach us. Have you imbibed that inconsiderateness already? Then know that something in you that belongs to the good person, to your better I, has died. Weigh it up whether you really can do no other and in so many cases you *will* be able to do otherwise and give up something that lies in your interest for the sake of another, perhaps for an unknown person who will never know what you do for him, to spare him pain.

"Woe to those who in daily life show too much heart," one usually says. Certainly they do not have it easy, and often they cannot pursue their own interests unfettered as another might do. They have not got the security and goal consciousness of the demeanor that belongs to success. But they know a happiness, which always remains hidden to others, and they have a deeper knowledge of life and of truth. Their soul and their heart have a part in their life, and love goes out from them.

Therefore, protect yourself against inconsiderateness

51

and seek the cases where you can withdraw from your unshakable laws. We must knowingly and unknowingly do the other person so much pain that every single case where we can deprive this way of acting to which we are condemned means a win that brings sunshine into our existence. And where we recognize in one or another of our efforts the happiness of the other, even when, according to the usual rules of the fight for our existence, we might put it aside, we recognize that we are there reconciled with humanity and rejoice. That is so even when we are only dealing with trivialities. And even if in the eyes of others you are regarded as impractical and no one thanks you, *remain as the inner voice calls you to be.*

6.

*So each of us shall give account of himself
to God.*

Now comes the third question: I get into
the situation in which I interfere injuriously in the life of
another person because I have *material interests* to
represent.

I lead a business and have in my employ a worker
who is not filling his place properly. The interest of the
firm in which I am employed dictates that I replace him
with a more qualified person. But he has a wife and a
child. Now I stand between the duty to represent the
good of the firm and the personal, human consideration
that obliges me to be indulgent toward the negligent
worker. Perhaps he drinks as well. But for the sake of his
poor family, and even though he never once thanks me
for this consideration, I am called upon to indulge him.

Or as a musician I lead a concert enterprise and have
to hire men and women as singers. After I have had them
singing every winter for years, others begin to notice, as I
do, too, that their voices are no longer so good. They no
longer please. The interest of the enterprise dictates that
I employ other, younger people. The interest of the singer
says to me that it is a cruelty if he is already receiving

enough cancellations and is coming to conclude that his voice is at its end. And now that I, too, point to his ruin, he sees glaringly before him the worries of what will become of him. I have lived through this despair with several previously famous singers and was always happy, I admit, if I did not have to determine who should sing or not. And where I have had to decide and had to choose between heart and reason, heart or justice, I have often suffered greatly.

Even in the most modest position, one comes into these conflicts. And the more comprehensive one's activity is, the more difficult they become. No one who acts in life fails to become guilty of interfering damagingly in the existence of other people and does not have to make decisions that mean a hurt for other people.

In the very fight for the good we come to the point where we interfere damagingly in the lives of people. I know that the influence of this or of that person is bad, and I recognize it with others as a duty—without my having anything personal against him—to be cold toward him and to cooperate in that which is undertaken against him. The purpose gives me the right. But I injure a person, and perhaps with the best of intentions I do him an injustice in many respects.

To be active beyond the borders of my own interests *therefore means to become guilty.* Whoever has not yet felt that has never sacrificed himself for something.

For that reason, we are not permitted to concur in every condemnation of men in leading positions of which we hear. We must take into consideration the responsibilities they bear and the necessity in which they find themselves to set the material interests above the human. People who live for themselves, who bear no responsibilities, who do not contend for the competent and the good (and thus, too, do not become guilty like those who stand in the midst of the fight and activity), do not know these conflicts.

When, however, you do experience the conflict between the material and the human considerations, you may not simply say, "I serve a business. My action is impersonal. Therefore I only allow the business responsibility to speak and am exempted from the human responsibility." Certainly those who do say that have things easier than the others and achieve much. They are also on legally unimpeachable ground. Their integrity and their honor cannot be doubted. But in order to be able to do what they do, they have killed personal morality, the truly human in themselves, and therewith the best in them is condemned to ruin. Man may never stop being human.

In all of your activity, you may *never be an impersonal energy, an organ of execution* of some sort of thing, *an agent of the society.* You must, rather, set your own personal morality over against that in all things, however uncomfortable, however embarrassing it is for you, and try, in everything you must do, to act according to humanity and according to your responsibility for the destiny that you are preparing for another person.

Is it necessary, is there no other way, than that I harm him? Is what I do to him really in relation to the material interest that is in question? Wrest from humanity the impossible, never be quiet, never allow yourself to have what one calls a good conscience. For the ethical person there is no such thing as a good conscience, but always only battle with oneself, doubting and questioning. Has the ethical person been what, according to the demands of deep-seated humanity, he ought to be? He worries that he forbids the ethical person in himself voice where he ought to have commanded it.

No one can decide for you. You must follow the

55

demands of the business dealing so far, and so far you may and must be led by considerations of personal morality. In every case, you must *decide for yourself*, without being able to avoid the dangers of erring on one side or the other.

But if you err, err rather on the side of the human than of the material. We children of our time are so accustomed to the theories of objectivity, which our generation is supposed to be absorbed in, that our human considerations in everything have receded. Only he manages to accomplish something who puts himself above everything else in a given moment, not from hardheartedness but from reflection. But know this: It is not just a matter of what we accomplish outwardly in the world but of what we give *humanly* in every situation. When you feel in a person that he is fighting with himself in order to remain a man in everything that he does, then you experience a sense of satisfaction and are reconciled with life. The discord, the self-division of the will to live that darkens the world for us, is lifted, only for a moment, only at one point, but lifted. The destiny of man to redeem is fulfilled. From such people there streams a power for good. Such people are able to do much that another, who does not fight for his humanity to the same extent, behind whom the person is not so sharing and so sympathetically forward-looking, is not able to do. Seek after them.

The opposition between material and human responsibility is not found in Jesus, because he looked upon the world as short-lived and attached no importance to working in it. Therefore he said to man: "Pull back from everything, hold yourselves pure from the world, throw off everything that can hinder and reduce your practice of personal ethics. Position yourselves outside the world."

For such people he has drawn the ideal of perfect personal morality.

To us, however, the voice of his spirit proclaims, in the time in which *we* live, that we are to engage in battle with the ideal of this perfect personal morality. We do that as active, working people standing in the world and defending it as the most precious one we have, as the energy of our souls. And, insofar as we are able, we are to fight to the utmost against the conditions we find and against what they dictate and impose. Moreover, in all our acting and doing we remain compassionate with people and can never be free of our personal responsibility as we work upon our fates.

To recognize the ideas of Jesus as the great, true necessity and to stand with them in the modern world and in action, like one who bears something precious on his head with arms lifted high through a torrential storm—that is what we ought to do.

7. FIRST SERMON ON PROPERTY

. . . those who buy as though they had no goods.

I COR. 7:30C, RSV

Every Sunday morning when I set out to address you on ethical questions, it almost seems to me as though I ought to apologize to you that once more I am delivering a purely didactic sermon. There are certainly some among you who came into this church seeking comfort and who thus will remain unsatisfied. I shall have forced your meditation onto a subject that is wholly distant from you. Nevertheless, I still feel the inner necessity, in this time I have with you, to get clear about many things that otherwise one brushes only lightly in a sermon. We are reflecting with each other in this way in order to try to become the people whom our times, with the many questions that they bear in themselves, need.

We have been reflecting in recent meditations about what we have to avoid if we are not to interfere injuriously in the existence of another person. Yet life, with or without our knowledge, continues to bring us to the point that we either add injury to him or hurt him. Then I attempted to sharpen our feeling of responsibility in all the questions that arise here. We begin today with the problems surrounding the help we owe to others. Indeed,

I shall single out the *problem of property*, the most topical and difficult of today's problems.

The question of property stands on the border of the questions that have to do with not damaging the existence of other persons. I say that because the one who has property, whether he owes that to his own proficiency and unimpeachable means or not, nevertheless is well-off at the cost of others. He gathers together in his hand what would otherwise be parceled out among several others. He possesses in proportion as others do without. On the other hand, the problem of property stands on that border in that it allows him who owns it to do good works for the needy and for every good purpose. How far is he who owns property obliged to utilize it in this way? The two great questions raised here, therefore, are: *In how far is property, viewed in general, legitimate?* And, *In how far is it destined to be utilized for the good of others?*

To both of these questions we seek in vain for clear and satisfying answers from Jesus that will show us the way in our judgments. You will have noted that from the passages I read to you at the altar. Jesus, like those around him, expected the end of the world in the immediate future. Therefore, all acquisition and possession had no meaning for him. Thus he preaches: "Gather no treasures for yourselves!" What a man owns is useless to him. Jesus does not preach that man should work and gain honestly just to manage to exist. This, too, fell under the concept of earthly worries that are no longer appropriate for him.

Among the first disciples, moreover, there was already an uncertainty concerning Jesus' position toward property. Both of the oldest Evangelists, Mark and Matthew, let the Lord combat only worldly worries. The

Evangelist Luke, by contrast, lets him utter hard words against the well-to-do. In the Sermon on the Mount, as Luke offers it, he allows the most frightful woes against the rich to be attached to the Beatitudes to the faithful. And often he has him speak as if the dispossessed stood nearer the Kingdom of God than those with possessions—which, I believe, did not correspond to the view of Jesus, who only saw the disposition of the heart and did not think so much about externals.

You often hear the expression *"Jesus was the first socialist."* That is at once both right and wrong, as is always the case when we take notions from our own day back into history and try to apply them to figures of the past. Jesus was a socialist insofar as he wanted to abolish property. But Jesus was no socialist, because he did not want, as modern socialism does, to create better economic conditions for the many from the property that the wealthy ought to give up. Rather, Jesus demanded it be given up for the sake of the soul of him who owned it. "Give away your riches, that you may have treasure in heaven!" Socialism says, "Work must correspond to more correctly and equally divided gain." Jesus, of course, did not pose the problem of work.

Through the fact that the end of the world did not come, even Jesus' view of property was confuted. The community at Jerusalem experienced that in its own body. Its first members determined that everyone should sell land and goods and that the money should be shared out among the whole body. The results were, first, that a conflict broke out between the old Jewish poor and the Greek-Jewish poor in which the one group maintained that the other was better provided for than they. Second, that Christians, as the story of Ananias and Saphira shows (Acts), succumbed to the temptation to defraud and did so, as they all shared out their belongings, because they held back a portion for themselves. Third, that the community became terribly poor and, under appeal to their prerogative as the oldest community, had to go begging among the rest of Christendom. In the letters of the Apostle Paul, you can read how he collected for the Jerusalem community in Greece and Asia Minor and brought them the proceeds.

It is *Paul* who took the lesson from this experiment in early Christian communism. He never challenged his people to divest themselves of property, but, rather, demanded that everyone work and earn in order to live independently and to be able to help those who were in need.

When we say "The ideas of Jesus concerning property are set aside through the failure of the end of the world, which he had awaited, to appear," we mean that only *outwardly*. The inward idea of Jesus, that we not be consumed in earning and possessing, that we must therefore fight to remain inwardly free from earthly goods, is valid for *all* generations. And that is true no matter how they stand otherwise on the individual questions of property. "Seek first the Kingdom of God and its righteousness" . . . "What does it help a person if he should win the whole world and lose his soul?": these are eternal expressions, which are the business of all of us. It is as if they were spoken only yesterday, *to us perhaps more than to any generation before us*, because, whether we want to be or not, we are so preoccupied with the material and are so dependent on it.

If this be presupposed, what is our position as to earthly goods and to property?

*　　*　　*

Albert Schweitzer

We differentiate two questions: Is property as such legitimate? And to what extent does the owner have the duty to use it for others?

The first question is really more a sociopolitical than a religious question and is usually so treated. If I dare to touch it lightly here in the worship service, that is not to take a position on this or that political-social view, which would not behoove me here and where views can differ.

I allude to it from two grounds.

First, the question of property today is so broached in all its magnitude that not only can it be considered purely religiously, but it must be overviewed in its whole extent. But then it is necessary to go back to the essence of property itself, for out of the essence of a thing we conceive what position we must take toward it.

What is the *essence of property?* How does it come about?

A person works a piece of land. Because he used his labor on it and procured the seed to make it fruitful, he says: "This field belongs to me. That is, I may harvest it, and I may recultivate it. When I die, my children may harvest and cultivate it." Thus began the possession of land.

A man worked in a trading business and gave valuables for it. Then he maintained that because he had done this and that work, this is now his and his heirs'. Thus arose capital.

Possessions or property are thus *accumulated work* and are *justified as such*. It is not only that, however. There is something more added: the cooperation of society. *Society* creates the ordered conditions that make it possible for the individual to retain what he has earned. It guarantees him that no one may come to him and say,

"I need what you have; therefore I am taking it." It guarantees to him that even those in the most extreme need may not take from him what exceeds his own needs, no matter how far it exceeds them.

Property is thus accumulated work that is guaranteed by society itself without consideration of the needs of the needy. There is something divisive in that. As accumulated work, it is justified; as guaranteed by society without consideration of the needs of the needy, it is *contestable.*

It is contestable, further, because the increase of property where it is once granted and is aided through circumstances no longer really represents a saving up of work. It is, rather, multiplied according to the law that Jesus once so expressed: *"Whoever has, to him will more be given."* And that, of course, has its complement: *"Whoever does not have, from him will be taken what he has."* Whoever inherits a sum from the work of his parents can possess and increase his property, without ever having performed work corresponding to his property, so long as he is clever and lucky enough to put his means in a good undertaking. *Others* now work for him. They work much, and many among them perhaps have scarcely enough to live from, while *he* is able to devote himself to pleasures and to doing nothing, if he likes. Nevertheless, he daily becomes richer.

That society guarantees property without consideration of the needs of the needy and that property is not only accumulated work of one's own but the exploitation and storing up of the work of others cause us difficulties. It is, on the one hand, something that is justified, as the accumulation of one's own work, but its justification is also doubtful for us if we are thinking people.

We cannot escape the recognition that in the final

analysis, society is the master of property. When required for the well-being of the general community, the community has the right to reduce individuals' property and to draw on it for itself. In the time of great misery that we face, it can do nothing else than to proceed so. It will tax property in unprecedented ways. Exploitation of the mined treasures of the land as well as many other things will be snatched from private control and saved for the state. An enormous evolution will take place in the coming years under pressure of circumstances, under pressure of need, and under pressure of ideas that come out of reflection concerning the essence of property. For both inward and outward reasons, that cannot be stopped. It will come with terrible injustice to those who own property and with terrible presumption on the parts of those who strut along preferring to talk instead of to work. Would to God that we had already experienced this transformation of relationships throughout the world and had survived the battles it will bring. As to how they are to be carried out, religion has nothing to say. It is a matter of choosing outward means that are appropriate to the goals, and that is something about which the members of a people must make up their minds.

[The exact working out of the sermon breaks off here. The conclusion is sketched in pencil in the margin, leaving the main portion of the page free for the fair-copy.]

SKETCH OF A CONCLUSION

1. Problem of property not abolished. Not nationalize everything. The boundaries of the economic, social

capacity of the state much narrower. Property remains without initiative. Socialistic ideals, communistic, if [it] realized in our society, so certain the ruin of the society as it [was] of the first Christian community in Jerusalem.

2. Outwardly, materialistically, not to be solved, but only through changed conviction in which owners make right use of their property, in which they recognize that in essence property is bound to justice, and in which they make good the injustices by placing property in the service of good purposes and of the needy. And the motive for this is not to do a good work as such, but under the pressure that comes from reflecting on the essence of property itself.

3. Property not only to own; [the owner] has it not only from his work, but from society. [Therefore] not to own property, but to be stewards of it in the sense of society. Contrary to the narrow conception of property. (That is mine. I may make of it what I wish.) That [is] the spiritual element from the reflection on the essence of property: all property belongs to society, even what I earn of it through work, for society first makes it possible. As such [we are] nonowners. Word of Paul, which hangs suspended over our consideration, expressed. (Next sermon: *Who then are the owners?*) He [Paul] [sees] it from the idea of the expected end of the world: The being of the world is passing away. As out of the essence of property itself [it is clear to us]: the only stance toward property. As those who have nothing, although they have and bear responsibility for what they begin for the welfare of others. *What that means for each of us.*

8. SECOND SERMON ON PROPERTY

Do not neglect to do good and to share what you have . . .

HEB. 13:16a, RSV

In the last meditation in which I spoke to you, we entered into the most difficult and timely question of ethics. We began to reflect with each other about property. Jesus, as we saw from the reading of the scriptural passages, gives us no answer to the question of property as we modern people pose it. He and those around him awaited the end of the world soon. Hence, for him, property, profit, and work come to nothing and only come into question as difficulties to preparing for the Kingdom of God. When Jesus teaches his followers and us that we must remain inwardly free from earthly goods, however, we then have insistent words in which he teaches us eternal meaning: "What does it avail a person if he win the whole world and for all that damage his soul?"

For us, however, as modern people to take a position toward profit and property, Jesus is of no help, because he does not presuppose our circumstances. We must rather reflect in an ethical spirit on the essence of profit and property in order to come to some clarity. Since we did that last time, let the question of the justification with which we say "That belongs to me" have the preponderance of our attention here.

We saw that the justified and the unjustified are all mixed up in the matter. Property is justified insofar as it is acquired through work, when it represents accumulated work. On the other hand, however, when I have possessions and see the need of the starving and in my hand the money increases according to the law "To him who has will more be given," I can again become confused and ask myself whether I may keep it. We must also bear in mind the other fact that it is society, with its ordinances and rights, that protects property and makes it possible at all.

I own property thus not only because I have worked or taken over the yield from the work of my parents but also because society gives me the possibility of keeping it. Thus society joins in all ownership as co-owner. All of the property that I own does not belong to me in the sense that I may say to myself, "That is mine. I can do with it what I want," but only in the sense that I say to myself, "That is property which I should administer in a profitable sense for the general public and for which I am obliged before my conscience to be responsible."

Property, therefore, means—and here we come to the question we have to take up for today—*responsibility.*

What ought I to do with that which I own? How far may I use it for myself? How far must I let it go to those who are needy?

First the question: *Who is an owner?* Who has to feel responsible for property that he has at his disposal?

Perhaps it has occurred to you that up to this point I have never spoken of the rich and riches, always only of owners and property in a completely general way. We do not want to fall into that cheap grumbling, which is often taken for religious, about how completely different things would stand in the world if the *rich* would only fulfill their duty to the poor. There are certainly enough examples of the fact that rich people often live withdrawn lives, concerned only with pleasure and luxury, without troubling themselves about what good they might accomplish with their means. But it is just as certain that everyone who opens his eyes also becomes aware of rich people who are conscious of their responsibility and quietly contribute much to the alleviation of need. When someone stands in front of me and inveighs against the rich, I find myself wondering whether *he*, were he suddenly to come into great possessions, would use them correctly himself. Often it is precisely those who have grown up in great wealth who have the most heart, while those who have only recently come into money are those who often think more about how they can enjoy their money.

Let's leave the rich therefore. We are not their judges, and let us rejoice in this hard world at every wealthy person who seeks to do good. *Let's speak about us*, the well-off and owners. For most of us, wealth and property begin where our means leave off. Whoever earns three thousand francs, with perhaps also a little set aside in savings, says to himself, "You are a worker or a craftsman. What you earn just reaches for your living needs. You aren't bound to worry about others. Leave that to those who earn ten thousand." And the person who earns ten thousand says to himself, "I have large expenses. What I can give up for others is not much. It scarcely comes into question. Yes, if I were like those who have one hundred thousand lying in the bank!" And they on their part say, "What is one hundred thousand these days? Money is worth less and less, taxes are constantly going higher, and finally one is counted rich and nevertheless has scarcely enough to live on."

Thus we speak from one ownership and earnings level to the other, and we lay the responsibility on those who are wealthier than we ourselves. And then we go on to fantasize about ourselves and what we would want to do "if only" we had more means. This *self-deceit* is the great enemy of reflection about the duties that are laid upon us concerning what we do with what we own and earn.

For that reason, the question *Where does property begin?* must be put in all sharpness. In equally sharp focus, the answer runs: An owner is anyone who, when he goes to bed in the evening, has something left over for the next day. Do not choose to regard that as exaggerated, as something that is perhaps logically correct while having no practical meaning. We ought, however, to regard it as the truth, which we do not like to understand because it is uncomfortable for us.

Where do you get the intrinsic right to go home evenings with money in your pocket when you encounter people on the street whose hunger shows in their eyes and who do not know how they will spend the night? Or you go into the street and see a person with worn-out shoes with holes in them wading through snow water, while at home you have a second or a third pair of shoes. And you say to him, "Let's see if we have about the same sized foot," and if it is about the same, "Come, and take the pair of shoes that I have in reserve."

Or you see someone in a torn suit in which he can never show himself to find work, and you have one which you don't wear. How may you pass him by and dismiss the idea of offering to him your other one because he has a ripped one?

Those are not exaggerated ideas. Woe to you if you have figured out such a comfortable, rationalistic ethic in which these questions of how you keep something for yourself while others have nothing no longer burden you. Woe to you if you do not seem bad to yourself, if you go quietly on your way! Woe to you if you are not tormented by memories of people upon whose encounter with you the inner voice said "You should help them," and when you delayed and reckoned to yourself that you were not really in a position to help.

Just as we experience the great daily wonders of light, of growth and so many other things no longer as mysteries because we continually experience them, so likewise we react to the great ethical questions. We feel them as what they are as they continually obtrude upon us, but we see them as questions that have found their obvious solutions in daily life. We treat them as matters over which we may now skip to the day's agenda. But just as only *he* experiences the things around him who experiences the phenomena of nature again and again as something wonderful, so only he also stands in the ethical life who is troubled again and again concerning the questions of whether and how far we may keep a reserve supply for now and the future when others need what we have and could give. Among the events in my life from which I cannot get free, allow me to give you a prime example so you will understand what moves me in this.

On an ugly winter's evening, I arrived in Paris and traveled, with my suitcase in front on the car, to friends with whom I was to get out and take lodgings. Two hundred meters from the house, a man began to trot along the sidewalk next to the car in hopes of being allowed to help with unloading and carrying the suitcase in. As the car stopped, the misery of this existence caught me: torn, hungry, frozen, wet through, and puffing, he stopped and wanted to occupy himself with getting the case. But the porter of the house, who in the meanwhile had come out, would not allow him to enter, for he did not look all that trustworthy. I could say nothing to the porter about that, for he was only following his instructions and I was a stranger in the house and had no rights. In haste I pressed a few coins into the man's hand . . . the heavy door closed, the trunk went up in the elevator, and I stepped up to the entrance hall. In the evening we sat happily together at the table, but I could not excuse myself for not having followed that inner voice. That voice had said to me: "That is your neighbor, sent by fate, whom you must care for with your means." I had excused myself by alluding to the circumstances and to the sense that my behavior might appear conspicuous and exaggerated.

If we dare to go into such memories that pursue us and to try to account for them, and to go into the questions that encounter us again and again in this way, then the normal and the rational appear to us as something untenable by which we want to delude ourselves. And the truth, that we also want to keep the little we have and want for ourselves, must be yielded. It falls on us like a pack of angry animals that surround us so that we can go neither forward nor backward.

No one finds the way to morality who only has the eyes of commonly accepted rationality, but only he who knows that he *also must do that which* to the common judgment *appears as exaggerated.*

Therefore, even if we belong to those who more or less live from hand to mouth, that which we save for ourselves from day to day or from week to week is not a self-evident right, as we like to say to ourselves, but something for which we bear responsibility and that we must give up when the inner voice calls upon us to do so.

Two forces work on us. The *one* is *naturalness*, the elementary co-experiencing and compassion with the other human being, which says to us: "You have still more. Therefore the other also should have." The *other* force is *rationality*, which says: "You must have something for yourself and for yours, which makes you and yours secure from day to day, so that should your income fall off, you will have something and protect yourself against becoming, through something unforeseen, yourself a needy person who is dependent on others' help."

There is truth in both forces. Both compete against each other. In this opposition, no decision can be given. Each must gropingly seek the way to his own responsibility and decide from one case to the other what he experiences as duty, as necessity. No person can expound it to another: "This you may sensibly keep for yourself, and this you must give away." *Everyone must settle it with himself.* But he is never finished with the question. Again and again, he becomes uneasy about whether he is fair with the responsibility that is laid on him with that which he owns and whether he does not forget to do good and to share, in the measure as it is decided for and by him.

It is decided for each person in a unique way. The one may profit, put property to property, in order to found a large works that offers many people secure bread. He must and ought to have capital so that his undertaking is assured and it can also hold out in times of heavy losses. For another it is decided that he should think less on the expansion of his property than on the best use of it. He can take it upon himself to use his property for good and for himself to lead a life so unassuming and modest that it stands in no relation at all to his property.

Here everyone must seek what is the best decision for him and obey the inner voice that speaks in him. For many, the word will and must become true: "Go, and sell all that you have." Here is a hurt that needs you, that needs your means. When there is no one who hears such a voice, there remains both among us and in far lands much undone that ought to be done.

And we may never become composed, but must always ask ourselves, "Is it *really* necessary and permitted, then, that you keep this for yourself instead of doing good with it?"

Whatever our decision may be, in practical life we all stand *again and again before the one question:* That is *surplus,* which could have been given to the poor! We buy a piece of furniture or a work of art according to our taste, we treat ourselves to a beautiful book, we celebrate a festival in the circle of our relatives, or we undertake a short trip for relaxation—and precisely when we want to be happy, the idea overtakes us: "What good you could have done with that! May you really use it in that way for yourself?" And don't knock this consideration dead once and for all; otherwise something in your heart is dead! Don't ban it from your house like an uncomfortably dunning bill collector, but let it come in to you, let your family, let your children, note that you think about such problems.

There are decisions that we can cheat on through appeasement: What we spend is not lost for the others, we say, but it represents a service that helps many to live.

Moreover, Jesus himself defended the *right of "sur-*

plus" and made it evident that there are cases when it is appropriate. When the woman at Bethany anointed him with spices, the disciples grumbled and complained that she ought to have sold the nard and given the money to the poor. But he said, "Why do you trouble the woman? She has done me a good work." A good work in that she showed him love with an intrinsically unnecessary expense. Thus we, too, have the right to act similarly toward our friends.

And nevertheless these decisions may not be allowed to lull us for the long haul; rather, we must remain continuously moved by the question. . . .

Therefore, what I say to you concerning property is necessarily unfinished and contradictory. On the one hand, property is a social necessity on which rest the continuation of society and the creation of normal and prosperous conditions. All spending makes work and earnings possible for others. Property is, however, simultaneously a keeping for oneself over against those in need. I can only repeatedly say to us all: *Everyone,* even he who only keeps a bit, *is an owner,* and he may not rock himself in peace, but must always be troubled about *whether* he can account for and *to what extent* he can account for his having something while others starve. Moreover, I can only say further that we may *not enclose ourselves in the rules of rationality* and say, "This and this I need for my life's maintenance, as I am accustomed to it, and for the securing of my existence and that of my family and those dependent upon me." Rather, we must presently have enough so as to meet the challenges to help that come to us from the inner voice, *unconditionally to give and to sacrifice what is demanded from us.*

Added to this necessarily incomplete and contradictory statement, I am going to give you *laws that are attainable for everyone* and that would represent a far-reaching solution of the problem of poverty, were they to gain general approbation.

The first is this: *Restrict your living requirements* so that you have something to give. *Review your life-style* and that of your family and see what you could save in order to be rich in doing good. And I say that directly to us who do not number among the wealthy and who so easily come into the temptation to say to ourselves that all that we have is necessary for us ourselves.

What the world lacks is not large sums that this or that rich person keeps but the many small gifts that those who possess little spend unnecessarily. Those are the water drops that ought to fill the stream to water the land.

And Jesus knew the people. What he expressed in one of the last of his parables, the parable of the ten talents, is touchingly true. He lets three men receive property from a master to administer and describes what they do: Two begin to do what they ought; the third is useless and buries his talent . . . and this third man is precisely he who has received least.

Stand for an hour at the door of a cinema and see who comes there bringing money in order to spend some time dully gazing at hopping figures on the white wall: people who live from hand to mouth, by the hundreds and thousands. What a lot of good could be done with the money that these people spend there day after day! And they are not people who do not know what misery is, who indulge in this little lifeless luxury. They are those who see what misery is when they cross the yards of the houses in which they dwell, who have dependents who are starving.

75

Therefore, for all of us, away with the lifeless super-fluities! Let's live as simply as possible so that we have something to give! If I risk saying this so urgently to you today, it is not only because the passion for squandering by those who live hand to mouth has risen immeasurably, like the misery of the starving, but because each can now easily and inconspicuously carry through a change in his life-style. On the one hand, the concepts of "in accordance with his rank"—which formerly held both great and small in tight constraint, were the cause of so much meaningless expense, and represented a hindrance for a return to simplicity—have, through the need in our times, which have thrown out so much of the traditional, been broken through. Moreover, we have known a displacement of property that has made modestly well-off people of many among the aristocrats and the rich. With that, a general challenge for a return to simplicity is set up. Take this to heart for yourself and for yours and make an end to the many unnecessary requirements so that you can help in the emergency.

I dare to set up another law that could be carried through by everyone and be of great importance for the general public if a number of people took it seriously. If you allow yourself something that is not essential to life but rather serves relaxation and satisfaction of the need for the beautiful and the nice, then take approximately the same amount it cost and specify that for good deeds. Do not spend more on such things than you allow for the welfare of others! If you undertake a vacation trip, then set aside a gift that will go to the poor and the sick to get them out of the muggy city air. If you make a celebration for your relatives or friends, then ration your means so that you can offer the hungry the same amount you enjoyed to help them. If you buy a piece of furniture or something else that gives you pleasure, think about granting something in the same value for those who lack the most necessary things, who do not know how they are going to pay their rent. And do this for all the amenities you do not begrudge yourself. I think that to a certain extent we must *share with the needy* in everything that goes beyond the essentials. We need to impose a voluntary secret tax through which we secure for ourselves inwardly the license to utilize for ourselves the property that comes into our hand.

When I say this, I also request those who are young and have no household to reflect concerning this secret sort of buying when they pick up those things that, in their lack of restraint, they select to make their lives attractive. When I see someone who, at today's prices, lights one cigarette with another and blows money into the air merely because he has got into the habit of it, I should like to have the right to go up to him and to speak to him. I should like to ask if he would like to set aside half of that for something that is urgent for the needy in order to lift the terrible immorality of his squandering. The same holds true for many other things where the young egoistically and thoughtlessly allow themselves luxury.

With that I have now given into our hands something firm and practical to help us find our way in a wide area of the confused question of property and the *use of property*. Let each of us reflect on it! *It can be carried through*, and if we take it seriously in life, we may hope to do something good and to compare to the man in the Gospel to whom his Lord said: "You have been faithful in little."

9. THIRD SERMON ON PROPERTY

And let us not grow weary in well-doing . . .

GAL. 6:9a, RSV

For two Sundays I have already spoken to you, in pursuance of our meditations concerning ethical problems, about property and about the responsibility that is given with it. We concluded from our reflection concerning its essence that we can no longer really conceive of property in the naive sense in which one says, "This is mine. I can make of it what I wish." We can only speak of a stewardship of goods in which society is *co*-involved in some way. And I must use it in such a way that I am conscious of the responsibility given with it, that it be useful to the general public.

How much of my property may I keep for myself?

In a certain sense this stewardship occurs sovereignly. No one may enumerate to the owner that he may use so and so much for his life-style, to what extent he may increase the property, to what extent he may give it away, and that he must make so and so much usable to the general public. In all things, he only has to follow his personal feeling of responsibility.

Where does property begin? we asked. Not, unfortunately for what my sense of my own comfort wants to dictate to me, always with those who have *more* than I. Succinctly put, *everyone* must regard himself as an owner who, in the evening, has kept something over for the morrow . . .

None of us, even he who lives more or less from hand to mouth, may find inward tranquility in this.

Reasonableness says to him: "You and yours, you must be secure for the next days in case your earnings cease or misfortune comes. For society, there must be enough working capital available so that it won't collapse with every difficulty that surfaces." The thinking heart says to us: "How may you have enough and have secured your future for yourself when others are now in misery?"

And no one can resolve this conflict. *We go about constantly making compromises.* We must decide individually each time how far we have to follow this rational dictum, upon which the economic life of our society rests, and how far we have to follow the heart and defend ourselves so that reasonableness does not once for all times triumph and thus free us from the terrifying question of how much of our property we may keep for ourselves.

In these reflections, I dared to emphasize that the misery in the world does not come from the fact that many rich people do not use their property appropriately. The misery in the world comes more from the many people who own little and earn modestly and who, because they are not rich, keep for themselves what they could spare for the good of the general public. For us, who belong to this class, I proposed two laws: (1) Your life-style ought to remain far enough within your means that you are rich enough to give; and (2) in that which you use for yourself beyond your real needs, for relaxation or pleasure, so order your accounts that you spend approximately the same amount for the needy, so as to share with them, to some extent, the right to use money for nonessentials.

Since we have spoken now of ownership and of what one should give up, let us think together today about *how we ought to give.*

"Let us do good and not become weary," says the Apostle. Doing good wants to be learned and reflected upon. Most people never come to the point of doing the good they really feel pressured to accomplish because they have no correct conception of doing good. They think it out like the hypocrite in them, who is intent upon magnanimous roles, intends they should. They are like the little boys for whom one has bought a fishing rod and fishhook. They stand on the water's edge full of zeal, thinking themselves able at almost any moment to catch a large fish. When a couple of hours have passed without results, they leave the rod lying there. Doing good is not something poetic, as it is often symbolized in pictures. It is something rather prosaic that requires perseverance and an idealism that has to contend with reality without losing its energy.

Our times require *two sorts of doing good* from us: the *impersonal* and the *personal.* The impersonal consists in our putting the means at the disposal of organized societies with which they can fulfill the charitable purposes they have set for themselves.

These societies are modern creations and represent great progress when one brings to mind the history of charity. On the strength of goal-conscious *organization*, they manage to do what an individual or many individuals working individually could not accomplish, and they seek not only to ameliorate the present misery but to obviate it. Therefore, give a portion of what, in your working out of your own sense of responsibility, you wish to use for the general public's good, to these societies . . . and do not wait until they seek you out, but seek them out!

The great danger for us modern people now is that we are too easily lulled to rest by the activity of a society and of the societies generally and that we too easily trust them with our responsibility. However correct it may be to say that through their activity misery has largely disappeared from the plazas and the alleys, it is a ready danger to us. Because we no longer see it, we think there is no more misery. Instead, we ought to seek it out, wherever it is, even when it no longer takes the clamorous and heart-rending forms it once had when it gave up exciting public sympathy.

But more still. We have a *false trust in the capacity of organizations to accomplish miracles.* An organization cannot accomplish more than lies in its nature.

In the first place, an organization is only set up to bring help in a series of cases that are approximately the same. The more idiosyncratic the circumstances of a case, the less likely an organization is in a position to dispatch it. *It cannot individualize,* so it then works either unsuitably or fails altogether. The societies are like watercourses that run through the land. Meadows that lie in between them remain unwatered, because the water must be led to them in small trenches.

That is the one point. Thereto the second: The charitable societies work *too slowly* for many cases.

81

Order demands that before help can be given, this and that inquiry be made and these and those papers procured. Otherwise the society cannot exist. But there are many cases where help must come *quickly* and without formalities or not at all. Many a person cannot take up the help offered by a society as he would like to simply because he has not got time to go from one office to another and to wait in each one until the line comes to him. And he also loses courage to do that. Whoever knows the conditions of the needy, whoever has seen how often a mother must leave small children alone at home in order to turn up at this or that office, knows how true this is.

In the third place, a society works with money that is entrusted to it. It may give support only where it knows that the help it supplies will certainly be brought to good use. It must be cautious not to risk something's being squandered. But in many cases one can help only if he can take the risk that the money will be thrown out of the window, and the support is hazardous. *So* to act is open only to the individual who makes the experiment with his own property.

In the fourth place, the help of an organization is too *impersonal*, too little human. Its work, in the final analysis, depends on some few people who, either as employees or as volunteers, stand at its service and represent the performing authorities through whom they work and have contact with the many who need their help. But these people do not have time to investigate those with whom they deal as they ought to. Moreover, they cannot maintain the spiritual freshness so to investigate them, so to listen to them, so to sympathize with them as is necessary, but rather something businesslike and cold comes into their procedures. Even with the best of intentions, they cannot be what they ought to be to those who come to them, and the work of the organization is commensurately degraded.

All of this only so that we do not indulge ourselves in a false security, where we say to ourselves, "The many fine charitable organizations among us will do the job. Everything is really well arranged." The reality usually just does not appear so good as one might assume from the printed yearly reports.

Have we not, in times past, seen that we have overvalued the performance of an organization in itself, to an overorganized state, in which the unsuitability of the performance comes to light with shocking clarity? Were not many organizations that we had created to meet the emergency of the time almost idling?

Every organization that is established as an embodiment of charity is, in the long haul, only worth as much as the capable human energies that are active in it. For it is *personal initiative*, the diversely flexible power of the individual, that is the unit from which each real performance is built up.

For that reason, consider first of all the fact that charitable organizations need not only your contribution; *they also need you*, your time, your work, your human mind. They all suffer from not having sufficient workers, people who undertake errands, who look after the needy, know them, feel and sympathize with them.

If you trace the history of charitable organizations, you can note how they accomplished much of a practical sort while they were still under the influence of their working founders. After a while they aged and still endure only from statutes, a yearly report, a committee, a charitable sum, an office, and some employees, because a rising generation of active people was lacking.

Albert Schweitzer

[The precise working out of the text breaks off here. On the next manuscript page, a detailed pencil sketch of the second part of the sermon follows, entitled "Concerning Personal Charity." In the shortest possible compressed form here we find what comes again and again to expression in Schweitzer's later utterances.]

SKETCH

Dispensing charity is a work

Work in societies plain work. Some sort of something for which you [have] qualification—. Not [required] to give, but *your time. Your leisure. Not keep for yourself!* Your humanity.
Thus impersonal giving without boundaries goes over into the personal.

Command of the personal (praise of private initiative). *On one's own responsibility.* And here not easy. Example of [the] thousand Francs. Speak from experience. Preserve a sum. "Use it for the best." [The] thoughtless giving. *Follow the person.* Example . . .

1. Time
With time and little means, much done. *Tact.* —Example of the neighbor who meets us, and no time. Here *example from Paris*, which stands in preceding sermon.

2. Religious freshness
Time and freshness: to (share) it with the other and to transpose yourself into [his] worries. And not only gift, but *worry*. Appointment.—*To be responsible*

84

for a person. To vouch for. Lend to him. (Now lend, who never before have lent.) Do not wait for the neighbor to be attacked by robbers and lying unconscious on the ground. Do an errand for him now.

3. *Do not seek the grand*
Not the grand gesture of help. That the merciful Samaritan proved [already] prepared to help; then [it is] self-evident to him that he cannot go by him and say to himself, "Someone else will come along; I am on a business trip."
Sermon on subsidiary office.

4. *Do not become domineering*
Rather be too credulous. Not to be domineering. Pride yourself on something; not to allow yourself to be deceived. Something defensive like police officials. Tanks. —Humanly: not to audit . . .

5. *Not become embittered.*
That is you. With what right embittered? *Not to become tired.* Throw money out. Case of vagabonds. Operated with letters . . . *What to do?* Money used up.—*Lift the condition of estrangement. That is you.*
The more [of the] person you accept, the less misuse. This man lives, that [he] gets charity, *in order to be free from it.* In order to rescue conscience. *"I have met with mercy, mercy of which I am not worthy"*: so say many, [when they] look back on their life. Society, which they as their enemy—[*sic*]

Conclusion
The problems only [to be solved] through the mind. People reconcile with property: Mechanical solution. *Fight between capital and work: [a] fight [that] both lose.* Mankind. *Create other atmospheres.*

10.

As each has received a gift, employ it for one another as good stewards of God's varied grace.

I PET. 4:10, RSV

Breaking into our series of meditations concerning ethical problems is Trinity Sunday. On this day, according to the usage of the Alsatian Church, the works of the Inner Mission are to be commemorated. This commemoration adds itself to the ideas that occupy us. What, then, is *"Inner Mission"*?

The name is not a particularly happy choice. It could be misunderstood as if conversion to the Church stood in the foreground. The Mission came into being in the first half of the previous century. The Christian Church then began to reflect on its social duties, in view of the misery that resulted from the complication of economic circumstances. As Jesus sent his disciples out to work among the heathen, the Mission is a sign that the Church also is determined to help in whatever emergencies occur among us. But the Mission stops short of becoming a teaching and sacramental institution, as it was under the old concept, and becomes an *organ of assistance*.

When the men who founded the great work of poor relief spoke out for the first time, this Mission sounded

86

somewhat revolutionary. Today it is, in principle, something that is so self-evident for us that we in the Church can no longer think otherwise. We only wish that in reality (in works) it accomplished still much more socially than it does accomplish and made Christians even a thousand times more actively relief-oriented people such as our time needs. Thus, as we celebrate the feast of the social activity of the Church, we should not think it sufficient to look back at the past and to enumerate what it has accomplished. We should look *forward* toward the great tasks that are posed for the spirit of Jesus in the present and the coming times. May we in our houses of God be grasped by the spirit whom the author of the first letter of Peter clothed in a wonderful saying: "Serve one another, each one with the gift he has received, as good stewards of the varied grace of God."

I think that through our observations in the previous sermons this word will reveal itself to us completely in its deep beauty. Today we rest from that before going forward on the next Sundays to reflect on additional ethical questions.

Serve one another! We started out from the elementary, fundamental principle of all ethics: reverence for life. For reverence for life, the sustaining and furthering of each being, as far as our sphere of activity can be extended, appears as a compelling challenge. Life for us means not only to experience our *own* fate but everything that occurs with other beings around us, with the creatures as with other people. We *share* it as a fate that is not strange to our own. We *empathize* with worry in worry, we *join* fear as our fear, we *assist* when an exertion is put forth to sustain or to advance and perfect life. To share experience means *to feel yourself responsible for everything* that happens within your reach.

Common sense wants to protest here that we are only responsible for that which current legal opinion claims we are. But the deeper, thinking conscience teaches us that the circle of our responsibility is not to be so staked out. Rather, we must live in a state of advanced uneasiness, whether, on the one hand, we have sided with the success of the good and the true, for the suffering creature and for people, as we ought to, and whether, on the other hand, we have always refused that comfortable saying "That is none of my business" when it wanted to disturb us where we could not give ourselves peace.

Thus we are drawn into a "service" without boundaries, as the fates that encounter us in life demand. None of us may feel himself free; rather, each has to help when the inner voice calls to him.

This serving is also at the same time a "working off," a retiring of an obligation. As we reflected about property, it became clear to us that no one may say: "That is mine. I can make of it what *I* wish." Instead, whether we have much or little, we always stand before the question How do you dare to keep for yourself and enjoy for yourself when others starve? And that which we keep for ourselves and for our enjoyment we must buy through that which we use for those who need our help. But that is not so for property alone! *Everything* good, *all* happiness, wants also to be worked off through that which we offer of it for others and for the public good.

The greatest good—and we usually value it too little—is health. You are robust and can work, as much as a person in your years can work. You have a good night's sleep and do not know the nights that, to wakeful people, seem endless and where one gets up mornings more miserable and battered than when one lay down in the evening. You have never experienced pain and suffering like others to whom a sickbed has become a trusted place and who can little more think of a life in normal health than others can of paradise. You have a healthy disposition that does not let the things that meet you make you sick, as do so many others who have sustained a less good balance from nature, and you do not react awkwardly and excitedly at every small thing as they do.

May you accept as natural all of that which you have as your share? No. Rather, you must also work this off through an act you offer in return for that. If you understand your good fortune, you can do no other than feel obliged to do something in return for it.

That for all happiness of ours a price must be paid through helping that you yourself create, that is deep knowledge of life, from which true happiness first comes . . . and in which we also become strong to prepare ourselves for "failure" and such suffering as may be allotted to us.

All help and work to which you can be called in life is *at once material and spiritual.* In that which concerns man, both always interpenetrate each other, since for man's life, as that of the highest being, both are involved with each other. Reverence for life, in respect of man, means not only the sustaining of his outward being and the furthering of it but that we cooperate in everything that is human life about us to bring it to its highest spiritual value, so that finally a perfect and happy humanity arises. That is what we experience as the world purpose in ourselves, the light from which some brightness falls on the darkness of being.

When an emergency presses a person or when he is in some sort of danger, he needs not only outward help but spiritual refreshment. This can only come to him, however, from the spirit of a person. Where this *total* help is lacking, nothing is really done. I spoke, in our last meditation, of how every good, in order to be able to serve purposefully and helpfully, must bind itself to a human energy. All the means that are available first acquire their true worth when appropriate people are available to take the time, the reflection, the research, in order best to use them. They are those who possess the heart so as to share the fate of those who are to be helped. They are those who don't wear themselves out where human goods are misused but confirm in love what the Apostle says: Love believes all things, endures all things, hopes all things.

All problems that need to be solved, the large like the small, *can only be solved through persuasive interchange* between individuals and between groups. It appears as if one wanted to solve all the material and social problems through a power struggle between capital and labor, on the one hand, and through the functioning of organizations, on the other. Where we find this conviction spread around in common "wisdom" and in the press, we must be frightened.

There is a wisdom that, although it has already been outlived, remains valid. From the *opposition of power to power* indeed come compromises from both sides that conform to the purpose. But an *agreement*, which means working together for a better future, will *never* originate out of that. This demands the creation of a reciprocity of trust that can only come from the encounter of both minds.

It is no different with *organizations*. They can indeed accomplish this and that, indeed a very great deal, toward bettering conditions. But organizations cannot accomplish the great and decisive improvement of which our time has need. That improvement, that great service which we need, can only be set in motion when more and more individual people, each according to the gifts that are peculiarly his, enter into it and become active in it.

What, besides all that is taking place now in the economic and social battles, must happen, if we do not want to fall into material or, less still, into spiritual misery, is for human nature to work itself out ever more richly. *This* is worth rousing. We who have seen through, comprehended, and want to be active in what is taking place must do all of this so that a new atmosphere, a quickening, warm, life-giving air comes in place of the coldness that currently surrounds us.

It is as if the Apostle were calling his "Serve one another!" to *us* as that generation whose salvation depends upon its grasping this truth.

With what can you serve? There is a great difference here between people. To the one, the chance to be part of the training and helping that is necessary is granted by his normal daily work; others are caught in a mechanical sort of work in which they cannot spend themselves as people.

As for the former, whether they occupy an office in the church or in the school or somewhere else where they can do people good, they must feel every day that they are favored, because even in their daily work they can do good to people. This is a great grace. One must always hold it up before oneself and find therein the energy for a joyous fulfillment of one's duty. What does it really mean that such people can say to themselves when they awaken every morning: "You may cooperate with the good in the world. What you are doing, everything, serves a great goal directly. You may spend yourself as a person!"

But what should the others do to whom no share in

91

such work is given, whose daily deeds consist in a mechanical work, in the service of some sort of machine, or clerical work or whatnot? This mechanical work, in which the person shuts himself off, poses a great danger; it is one of the givens of modern economic life. The person is impoverished inwardly and pulls back into himself. He loses the notion that he, as a person, *also* has something more to do.

Therefore, may the longing be kept awake for all and the conviction that they as people also have something to give to the world. I indicated that already in the conclusion of the last meditation when I said that everyone, in addition to the vocation by which he secures his living still somehow must seek an occupation in which he as a person serves people. If this longing is kept awake in him, then it will not happen that he will lose his connection with the world and its need outside himself. He will not pull back into himself in a long process, as does occur in thousands upon thousands of cases. In our vocational efficiency we may not do enough and then declare to ourselves, "We are useful members of human society," for to that belongs intrinsically *that as people we are something for other people.* So we must come out of ourselves, out of our vocations, out of our environments, and also be useful in human fashion somewhere and somehow.

Everyone can find that. He must merely seek, wait, and begin small. Like the workers, whom, according to the parable of Jesus, the master sought for his vineyard, who stood around watching to see if anyone came to hire them. So seek quietly and modestly where God can use you and do not become tired in waiting and seeking. For if the word of Jesus—"Whoever seeks, will find"—is correct anywhere, it is here. You will discover where you can serve and experience the blessedness of this service.

[On the border of the first manuscript page is found the following sketch of a second draft of this sermon.]

SECOND SKETCH

1. Feast of Inner Mission. Bad name. The concern [means] everything: [the] *physical and spiritual help.* Relief = to care for and to provide for. Encounter with our ideas. Called forth through the plight of modern conditions.
2. Reverence for life: *responsibility for physical and spiritual on a higher level.* The concept of life is expanded.
3. All *distress* physical *and* spiritual.
4. All *help* physical *and* spiritual. Begun to reflect concerning the neighbor: concerning property. At the same time however the *person* came into view. Time. Freshness. Friendly being.
5. Goods, with which we have to serve, not only money, but time, health, gifts, happiness. Spend of that for the world: a pound, with which [we] [have] to make the most.
6. The large question, *How much of my happiness may I keep?* The answer: compassion . . . service.
7. The generality of the word. *Experience it as possible, to be able to be something for others.*
8. The difference in the activities. I have gone out empty. The great spiritual danger.
9. *Whether God hears prayers.*

11.

Let all men know your gentleness.

In our last meditation we summarized *the general principles* we had realized together in our reflections on ethical questions. Today we go forward on our way and pass *from the general to the particular.* A perfectly daily question, which has certainly moved you in various ways already, will occupy us.

As a point of departure, the splendid word of the Apostle Paul is chosen: "Let all men know your gentleness." It expresses what I in my own words declared when I said that we must always, when the moment and occasion require it, practice our humanity and be compassionate and helping people for others.

We accept that this has now become self-evident, and in our collective reflection it has become still more obvious, so that we are resolved in the future to put it much more seriously into practice than in the past. But then our good will, especially if it wants to behave that way in the little matters of daily life, has to set itself in opposition to the customs and the habits that exist there for *social intercourse.* These customs and habits set up barriers between us and try to prevent our letting all men know of our gentleness. To many toward whom our

94

hearts drive us, they say, *"This is unbecoming,"* or, "This could be importunate or appear conspicuous." But we all stand so very much under the influence of the current views in such things that in many cases we do not do what we have it in our hearts to do.

The rules concerning politeness and decorum are to blame that people often pass one another by, strange and cold, and deny each other what would be ethical and natural, when inwardly they don't want to.

One *example* for many. In the next house lives someone whom you have known by sight for years. One day you meet him in black and with a sad face. Your inner feeling says to you, "Go to him and ask him whom he has lost and express your condolences to him." But just as quickly the objection comes to you that you have never spoken to him and thus have no right to address him. So you suppress what you want to do, and a ray of affection that would have helped another person does not light up the world.

What have religion and ethics, now, to say to the manners that hold sway among us? How far should the good that lies in them be respected, and how far may we set ourselves over them if they hinder the expression of true humanity?

The unwritten laws to which we all feel subject one summarizes under the word "politeness." Originally politeness designated the fine, customary behavior at a court, in differentiation from the untrained naturalness of unrefined people. As this naturalness has its good and bad sides, so also has its opposite, politeness. The naturalness of ethics carries with it the danger that tact and reserve do not get their appropriate due; the refining of ethics leads easily to externalization and to unnaturalness, which fight against ethics.

95

How does the politeness that holds sway among us stand in this regard?

The laws it raises up comprise *three kinds*: They ensure that we show esteem for the people with whom we have to do. At the same time, they enable us to deal with acquaintances in the nicest and friendliest ways. Third, they command us to observe a measure of reserve. All of the commandments of politeness can be placed into these three classes.

For both of the first two, the argument with ethics can be suitably dispatched. Our politeness is nothing less than healthy. What is admissible in the limitation of esteem is set by usage in our exaggerated expressions. If we write to a man whom we take at best for halfway honorable, we must entitle him "Highly esteemed Sir." "Honored Sir," which is in itself rich enough, he might find insulting.[1] If we use "Dear Sir" in order to avoid the embarrassment of attesting an honorific situation in empty words, it will, under some circumstances, be taken badly against us as an unwarranted familiarity.

How stupid this honorific business, which is prescribed for us, is, is also shown when we ought simply to go through a door! Each must act as if he counted himself unworthy to cross the threshold with the other at the same time. Hence, one insists that the other indeed go first, as if the witness of deference in such laughable minutia were something so terribly important.

---

1. *Translator's note:* Unlike English, the German language has a plethora of forms of honorific address for correspondents. Some of these are translatable; some are not. English has no equivalent for another example Schweitzer gives here: *Mein Herr*, which, under the circumstances he is describing, he notes, "passes for almost insulting."

Because custom does not allow us to halt within natural borders in expressing respect toward others, it forces us into lies and hypocrisy in small matters of life and corrupts our characters.

It is no different with the expression of friendliness. Here, too, the current politeness demands too much external in that it imposes upon us conventional flattery, hypocritical interest, and empty compliments.

The time will come in which politeness in these two points will be *simplified*. We ought already to try this simplicity now. But destiny and cleverness must be used. Clumsy rebellion is useless.

Let us recognize *what is legitimate in the current prescriptions*! They require that we control ourselves in every moment and that we are not to be respectful or friendly or unfriendly and disrespectful according to our moods. We are able to do that only if we subject ourselves to these set forms. Furthermore, these rules, however overblown they may be, contain an *indication of something valuable that underlies them*. They challenge us to allow esteem and friendliness also to acquire their rightful place in our real disposition. The politeness of the form should hold us to politeness of the heart. In the interpenetration of both arises true politeness, with which the exaggerations of the forms wither of themselves. In this way, for the individual as for society, the recovery of politeness is to be sought. Merely to criticize the ridiculous and the hypocritical aspects of this or that stupid form accomplishes little.

Ethics thus does not need to regard the fight against the current prescriptions of respect and friendliness as something pressing, because these, with all their misplaced emphases in particulars, are not able to stem the recovery of a politeness of the heart. It is different, however, with the prescriptions of the third sort that have to do with the degree of reserve that is to be observed.

The necessary and justified aspects of these prescriptions may be fully recognized. We live closely pressed up against each other, and it is *impossible to establish a relationship with all people* who encounter us or to allow them to come into relation with us. It simply may not be permitted by everyone, just as it pleases him, to be free to approach any other person, to speak to him, to take up his time, to tell him his opinions, and whatnot. Respect for the neighboring person requires that we *not obtrude* ourselves on the stranger. And we should be able to expect the same from others regarding ourselves.

These laws naturally may not be expanded further than protection against importunity requires. Like all principles of politeness, they are found among us exaggerated into external and unnatural arenas. We judge ourselves reciprocally in an almost ridiculous way as strangers approaching each other, even where circumstances for our getting acquainted in some way or other urge or simply demand precisely that we do it. A friendly fate can bring us together for hours with a person for whom we have interest and empathy, just as he feels for us. But etiquette wants us to act as if we were wholly indifferent to each other because we have not previously met and there is no one around who can take over the office of introducing us. Or a man with whom we are previously unacquainted, as in the prior example of our neighbor, is in a situation that arouses our sympathy. We would like to express that sympathy to him, and it would do him good to receive it from us, but we don't know each other and go along intimidated, as if we had paid no attention to each other, one passing the other by. A person, as it happens, could use our help, and we would gladly offer it to him. But we do not dare because he, according to the current rules of propriety, might believe we wanted to obtrude ourselves upon him. Or we on our side have need of his help and feel that he would gladly do that which is necessary. But we do not dare to request it, and he likewise does not offer, and we go away from each other as if we had remained totally oblivious of each other.

The principles of the politeness of reserve thus so often allow us, as everyone has already experienced a hundred times, to suppress an impulse for the politeness of a friendly advance and to persist in strangeness, even where we could and should turn others from strangers into acquaintances, from remote people into neighbors.

The damage goes still further. That the heart on so many occasions must keep still causes our notions of what ought to count as natural affection slowly to become falsified. We get accustomed to the fact that indifference will be shown to the stranger, and we relate to each other no longer as feeling people but as impersonal things.

This development has made worrying progress in the last decades. In place of the natural heartfelt politeness that our grandfathers recollected as an ideal, today the ideal everywhere is that of the gentlemanly *politeness of coldness.* The forms that ought to regulate a considerate reserve toward the stranger have become, through senseless exaggeration and externalization, formulae of rejection. In a correct way, silently or with words, to give the stranger with whom we come together somewhere to understand that he is nothing to us and should not have the temerity to want to be something—this is the essence of the politeness that, condescendingly, seeks to prevail as superior to the earlier, better ethics. It has already infatuated many circles.

As often as I find myself through circumstances in an exclusive hotel, I shudder at the inconsiderateness and lack of culture that the average one of these guests, in their elegance, displays. For days on end they live under the same roof, residing room on room, eating table on table, without greeting each other when they pass on the stairways and without taking the slightest regard when an occasion would demand it. How very much they are imitated one can see in so many young people of all classes, who, in their own environments, represent the same indifference and inconsideration toward the stranger. They do that as an achievement of modern education and have no little pride in their slick freshness.

Botanical scholars have shown that the water pest, the plants that so impede our still and our flowing waters today, did not always exist here. They first spread into our areas a relatively few years ago and, already ineradicable, expand from year to year, to our detriment. At the same time, the harmless water plants that formerly prevailed are being displaced. What is happening here in nature is, in principle, what can be pushed through in manners. Hence, it is so timely that we ask how religion and ethics stand toward the current forms or toward the politeness of coldness that is struggling to become current. What does the spirit of Jesus, the sure leader in questions of the relation of man to man, say to us?

Politeness consists of form and spirit. The spirit is the essential, the form the nonessential.

According to its essence, politeness is nothing other than the tactful practice of ethics and humanity in daily intercourse with known and unknown people. *It ought never to become empty form.* Training for politeness is above all training for natural humanity. This is the principle according to which you yourself develop and according to which you educate those who stand under your authority. In the face of the spirit of the times, be conscious of the fact that politeness does not come from the learning and recognition of so and so many rules of manners but must preexist these as a sensitive, obliging *disposition of the heart.* It acts with those rules as music does. The capacity to create melodies is not awakened through learned rules. They only serve the purpose of giving the tone line, which arose out of the inner creative impulse, its most perfect form.

The ideal of politeness, as it hovers before the inner man of all times and of all levels of education, and always shall, covers itself thus with the words of the Apostle: "Make your gentleness known to all men"—to all men, also to the stranger. An introduction of politeness that is not rooted in living ethical views is a loss for the society in which it comes to currency.

How far, now, must the politeness of a friendly advance submit to the existing commandments of *reserve* in our time? These are, on the whole, binding, since living closely together and having daily contact with many strangers makes it impossible, generally, for us to relate to them as anything other than strangers. But this strangeness may not become something self-evident. I must always be sensitive to it as something enjoined upon me. My heart should rebel against it and hold me to showing interest in every person. As circumstances permit, I may and ought to reject the unnaturalness of strangeness.

This goes right from the *greeting*, this most modest

and restrained form for lifting the strangeness between a person and me. In a city it would be pointless were I to greet everybody. I have to restrict myself to my acquaintances. But if I am where the people standing around me do not say Du^2 to each other or hasten by me, then inner politeness requires that greeting every man come into its own. If I go through a village, if I meet people on the highway, if I climb into a train compartment, it should be natural to me, even to the stranger, to let him know that I wish him a good day, that he is a person and not a thing for me.

If the natural politeness of greeting has receded so far into disuse, then city dwellers, and especially those who live in large cities, bear the largest blame. With themselves hindered from greeting the stranger, and in their thoughtlessness no longer finding this unnaturalness unnatural, they succeeded in letting the greeting remain repressed even where it was possible and appropriate. If they come into the country, they bear with them the city's impoliteness of nongreeting as modern behavior and its condescending tone. Their example finds approval, especially among the younger generation, because the people of our day have a sickly fear of not "going with the times" in everything.

---

2. *Translator's note:* English, unlike many other languages, uses the same pronoun for both polite and familiar address. German not only has a special form for familiar, intimate address, but that form reflects a sharp sociological difference between those with whom you would use only the polite form and those with whom you would use the familiar. The use of the *familiar* form, *Du*, would be restricted to family, children in general, and a small circle of close friends with whom you had a mutual agreement that you would *Duzen*, or say *Du* to each other. Schweitzer's allusion here refers to his assumption that the people he would be encountering were casual strangers to each other and that he would not be breaking in upon a "private" conversation.

In a remote little valley of Switzerland I had the occasion to trace how such omitting of greetings came about. Some twenty years ago a hotel was built there in which, from the second year of its existence onward, I met together with some friends from a large city for an extended stay at the end of each summer. During the first two years, all of the local inhabitants greeted the hotel guests in a friendly fashion. The guests accepted that as something obvious by such naive and backward people and probably thought also that it was their money, their beautiful clothes, and their high social rank that evoked the greetings. The responses had from most of them a smattering of condescension, if they were not almost inaudible or omitted altogether. Many times I pointed out that we hotel guests did not have to await the greeting of the country people, but rather, because we were guests in their region, we first ought to offer them a greeting, but my suggestion was regarded by most guests as my personal idiosyncrasy. The education of the big-city people went so far that, apart from two or three families, they didn't even hold their children responsible for greeting the adults among the country people first. What had to come, came. After ten years, the country folk scarcely greeted the hotel guests and accustomed themselves to their also going by others in silence. Then when a lady, whom I had met in my first year there, got angry that the country folk had given up their earlier, pleasing politeness, I was able to answer her: "They are simply going with progress and have learned from the hotel guests."

It is important, therefore, that we not be confused by the forms of manners of the modern spirit of coldness and of thoughtlessness and that we preserve the politeness of the heart in greeting every person wherever this can be carried through. That we wish each other a happy day from one person to another has a deep meaning.

With a greeting, a person lifts the veil of strangeness for a moment. From a distance, he makes acquaintance with a stranger without giving additional consequences and without awaiting a more fulsome approach by him. *Under what circumstances may I make a further step?*

Here we must distinguish between sure and less sure cases.

I have the right, without consideration of any sort of prevailing form, to lift the strangeness between a person and me as soon as I am certain that he needs someone's help and that I can be that someone.

If I go into the underpass of a rail station next to a person who is carrying a heavy bag, I may offer to grab on with him, whether he is wealthily or poorly dressed and whatever class I belong to. If I believe he needs advice or information, so as not to be injured from lack of knowledge, I may offer my service to him. If I come upon people who, with the approach of a thunderstorm, are trying to bring hay or sheaves to cover, I may offer my help. If I hear that someone who lives in my neighborhood needs a ladder or a tool that I happen to own, I may propose to him that he borrow it. If there is a sick person somewhere whom something that I have could serve, I may seek to ask whether I should send it to him. In a word: As soon as a stranger needs my help, or I can do something good for him, I may step out of my reserve.

May I also do that if it is not a matter of helping in an external deed, but if I only have more the impression that as a sharing person I could be something for the other person? This case is not so clear. Here I can more easily be in error or more easily be misunderstood than in the other situations. Consideration before approaching someone and caution in carrying it out are mandatory. But in spite of all doubts and hesitations, the rule should be valid, that when our heart moves us to show interest and sharing to a stranger who has aroused our attention in some situation, we should *do* this, come what may.

In a night express train that was due to reach Strasbourg toward the break of day, some ten years ago, I saw, upon awakening, an older man across from me who must have come aboard while I slept. He did not have a bearing that invited the contact of a conversation, but looked rather unfriendly. But a vague guess urged me on to strike up a conversation and to show him friendship. With that, it came out that he had been called to Strasbourg by a telegram. His son lay in our local military hospital struck down by a bad case of typhus. It happened that I could offer him much more than sympathy: Not confident in the city, he was happy that I accompanied him for the morning on the right way to the hospital, since no trolleys were running yet, that I helped him carry his things, and that I secured him accommodation.

Most complicated are the cases where the person wants to give up his reserve not in the interest of the other but in his own interest.

I have been in situations in which the strangers around me could have performed a great service for me with some sort of small help. May I approach my fellow passengers in a train compartment for a knife or a piece of string when I cannot otherwise help myself? Or I am passing by a property on which apples are being picked up. I am thirsty and have a great desire for one or two of these fruits. May I ask for one? I need information. May I approach people who are near me and could perhaps give it to me?

Let a word of Jesus from the Sermon on the Mount be

thrown onto the scales here: "Ask, and it will be given to you: seek, and you shall find; knock, and it will be opened." On the power of this saying, we may turn to strangers when we need someone and ask whether one of them wants to be a neighbor to us in the matter that we raise. We may do that despite the considerations that we alone could raise from our side, wanting to hold us prisoner to an anxious reserve.

But what about the cases in which I don't require a person out of some sort of need but only trace a longing to get acquainted with him, to get something spiritual from him, or to let him know of some sort of ideational kinship that exists between us? How many people, to whom we were attracted, have we passed by because, from fear of appearing importunate, we have not risked the small step toward getting acquainted! Have we always acted correctly in allowing shyness to triumph? Is there not something that rules in the impulse that lets us seek the acquaintance of people who come near us, which stands higher than all principles currently in vogue between people?

Therefore, in all cases that can come into question for *giving up strangeness* between people, I dare to break through, for we are much more natural and much more affectionate than is either useful or allowed according to the current rules. If we have the feeling that we can be something to a person, whether through outward help, through friendly sharing, or if we need him, whether for help, for sharing, or finally, if we feel impelled to come nearer to him, to give him something of our being and perhaps to receive something of his—we may always see ourselves as masters over the forms that want to hinder us.

Often there is something mysterious in the little things that pull people together. It can happen that the person with whom you become acquainted, if you make use of the opportunity to come closer to him, will become loving and valuable to you for your whole life. To whom do we owe our closest and most faithful friends? Accidents of life that once got us acquainted or words and deeds that we, following an inner impulse, risked toward them. The other aspect, which then created the constancy and depth between us, came from itself after the first contact had once taken place. To have people in life who are dear to us makes up the richness of existence. Often we remain poor in people where we might have been able to find some who would have been much to us. Why? Simply because we left unused, in passing, the circumstances that brought us so near, that we needed only to stick out our hands toward them.

And *what sorts of experiences* do we have when we dare to be natural and affectionate? Thoroughly encouraging. The other person does not misunderstand our crossing over the dug trenches but rejoices in it. Often he has desired it silently from his side. If one dares in passing by to ask for an apple, the one behind the fence had often thought to himself: The man outside there would certainly like one. If only I dared to offer him one! Everyone can relate something of such a noteworthy meeting.

One morning I sat somewhat bad tempered in a hotel in Barcelona. At an organ concert the previous night, I had missed very keenly the help of a good register puller and was reflecting in vain on whom I might secure for this office for the two remaining concerts. At the same moment there was a knock at the door, and a very shy man pushed through the door into the room. He began to apologize up and down that he had dared to seek me out, a stranger, and outside the usual times for visiting. He was a teacher's son from the Rhine, had played a bit of organ himself, was now in Barcelona as an engineer, felt alien, had a longing once again to touch an organ, and had for that reason, on the previous evening during the concert, decided to look me up. I was happy to excuse him the importunity; he could do no other. Beyond that I could say to him in good conscience that he came to me as someone sent. That same evening we practiced on the organ. He performed his task excellently. I was able to get permission for him to play on the organ of the concert hall whenever he wished. For his part, he undertook to maintain the organ and to repair its damages, which no one else in Barcelona was able to do. The directors of the choir and orchestra became his dear friends, so that he no longer felt alone. I myself with every visit to Barcelona became closer and closer to him. So for a whole series of people a service was accomplished and a spiritual quickening prepared simply because a shy person, for a moment, as from an inner instinct, had overcome his reserve.

Last autumn, still weakened from an illness, I came into Strasbourg by the last train before midnight. Trolley, car, or porter were no longer to be had. So I tried to pull my two heavy suitcases home. Before I had made three hundred meters, by setting the bags down often, it was clear to me that it was impossible. I decided to take heart and to ask the next passerby who overtook me whether he was going in my direction and in that case if he could help me with the carrying. A man sauntered by. I let him go in order to see if he turned right or left. He however went irresolutely farther, looked at the stars and then into the Ill [River], as if there below he saw something very interesting. A curious person, I thought, but still called to him finally. He came quickly and heard my request. Then he smiled and said: "I have been walking behind you since the train station and considering whether I might dare to offer you my help in carrying. I was about to take courage just as you came to me." So we two went through the night with the luggage philosophizing about how much love in the world remains suppressed through the false shyness of the needy and of those who could help. Encouraged on both sides by what we had just experienced with each other, we each made the decision to be natural toward people in all life's situations.

Everyone, who will only dare to do it, can have the experience that the approach to strangers, when it really is suggested by circumstances or arises from true interest, will be misunderstood as importunity far less than we fear. Instinctively, the other person senses that curiosity and tactlessness are not in play here and is forthcoming even when he does not completely understand us at first and we behave more or less awkwardly. There would be far more love among people evident if hearts were more courageous.

Some years ago a religious paper carried the following story: A Parisian trolley conductor was asked by a passenger of his car why he looked so sad. To that this response: "You are the first person with heart whom I have encountered today. The whole day long I have discharged my service and not been able to master the pain. I have a child dying at home. You are the first who has seen that I am sad and who has said a comforting word to me. For the others I was not a person, but only a man who had a service to perform." To this incident, the newspaper added observations on the heartlessness of people. That was wrong. Probably his *Du*-friends[3] among

---

3. *Translator's note:* See note 2 above. The reference is to the conductor's intimate friends.

the passengers were touched by the expression of pain, but they had not the courage to speak to the man out of anxiety about receiving the answer: "What business is it of yours what face I make?"

Whoever practices natural affection will certainly also experience *rejections*. We can hit upon people who possess no sense for that which authentic humanity offers and allows and who, perhaps, are also in that moment irritable and bad tempered. It can also be that they are so taken up by a worry or a sorrow that initially they simply wish to remain completely on their own and not to receive comfort. But these cases will always be exceptions.

If we experience a rejection with our good intention, there is nothing for it but to accept it without further comment and not allow it to make us despondent about future opportunities. What good, following the true spirit of morality and lifting ourselves in decisive moments above the current customs, we can do to people in our life and are able to receive from them is well worth the price that here and there the so-called disgrace of a rejection is also part of the bargain. No one can act as Jesus would have done without giving offense to the world.

Thus the politeness that religion and morality offer is in many senses a *different* one from that which wants to win through in the formulae taken over and expanded by our generation. In small matters we yield smilingly to that which outwardly is in force, as Jesus also recognized the rights of customs and submitted to the externals. But when the circumstances demand the inner politeness, we must obey the spirit of the true humanity. *Where principles and heart stand in conflict with each other, let us make the law of the spirit free from the law of principles.* It allows us to let our gentleness be known to all people to whom it could do some good and to await the same from them, without allowing ourselves to err, through that which condemns us in ordinary life to estrangement overagainst each other. So let us dare to strive to become sensitive, natural people and to proclaim and to live the Gospel of hearty naturalness of which our world is in such need. This will only serve to lead on the new mind of humanity.

12. DOUBLE SERMON ON GRATITUDE: FUGAL THEME AND COUNTERTHEME

Be thankful in all things . . .

I THESS. 5:18

I

The adage "Ingratitude is the reward you get from the world" expresses a sad truth that everyone has experienced. These words contain more than a simple observation that the world is in the habit of repaying kindness with ingratitude. There is also here an echo of the idea that "there is thus no sense in doing good." That is the tragic part. Due to the prevalence of ingratitude, much in human hearts remains unsatisfied that could in fact be satisfied. Because of ingratitude, much good that might be done is held back. *Ingratitude inhibits the spirit of ethical action in the world.*

Of course, when people agree so readily with the pessimism of the adage, they are not always being wholly honest. When we speak of ingratitude, have we always sought only that sort of thanks that we are entitled to seek as ethical people? Let's be truly open with ourselves. Often when we are disappointed in receiving no gratitude, we should not have been expecting any, or at least none of that sort. For all of us there is a great temptation here to use the good we do as a snare to entrap another

112

person. "Don't you remember what I've done for you?" we say to him when he once disagrees with our opinion or does not want to do what we demand of him. And so we drag him around behind us on a lasso of gratitude until he can take no more. If he defends himself against us, we call on our acquaintances to attest to his ingratitude. They, of course, agree with us and help us humiliate the other person. We are then filled with holy indignation.

But what is really happening? *You yourself* have sinned against gratitude much more than the other person, for you have *misused* it and have practiced extortion with it. Each of us has fallen into this temptation because here ugliness confronts us in such an honorable form and poses as something so virtuous that we fail to recognize it for what it is. It can even happen to us that we press the person who is obligated to us to act out of gratitude against his own conviction and conscience without our even being aware of it. So beware. If you are indignant at the ingratitude of others toward you, step aside a bit and ask yourself softly whether in the court of an ethical conscience it really is a valid demand for gratitude. And think about what you yourself have suffered when people demanded gratitude from you and humiliated you.

Still other demands for gratitude made by thoughtless people must be rejected by the ethical person. For instance, the silly and superficial things you attach to the good you do. When we have performed a service for someone, we insist that they should *give us a good reputation with others*. If they don't do this loudly enough, we regard it as ingratitude. Thus, when you are about to refer to the proverb "Ingratitude is the reward you get from the world," be sure to check whether or not

113

it is vanity in you that raises its voice the loudest. If you can be honest with yourself, you will often find that that is the case. Then bid vanity to be silent and revise your expectations concerning what claims to gratitude can be made. Take warning that generally it is thoughtless people who complain the most about ingratitude. Those who think clearly about the ingratitude they encounter do not find it so easy to make shrill noises of indignation.

Granted, however, that we have trained ourselves no longer to allow the ugly, the vain, and the superficial to participate in our expectations of gratitude, and granted, too, that we have been so successful in our efforts at self-purification that we really try to do the good for its own sake and not in the hope of some sort of recognition, we shall nevertheless still be hurt through the prevalence of ingratitude. What people can and ought to give one another in terms of reciprocal gratitude is more than mere satisfaction of more or less justified and pure expectations. Such gratitude as we do meet helps us to believe in the goodness in this world, and thus it strengthens us to do good. It is of no use for us to try to defend ourselves against ingratitude. The disappointment that touches our soul weakens us. Good seed sown in good earth sprouts in all weather, yet its growth in good weather is different from that in bad. We all have difficulty holding fast to the optimistic world view that empowers us for goodness. That is why ingratitude, which constantly robs us of our enthusiasm, is one of the worst powers of evil in the world.

We all have a part in this evil. We refuse to give one another *that which could reciprocally help each other.* Thus it is not just that we refuse to show gratitude because it seems to require some effort on our parts. We fail to give even that which is expressed in thoughts and words and small acts of kindness and which is not difficult for us. We are able to create for each other much satisfaction without much trouble and with a little attentiveness, but we fail to do it. Therein lies the problem.

When are we *habitually ungrateful*?

Were someone to say to us that even we belong among the ungrateful, we should probably get angry. Of course we can all remember occasions when we acted ungratefully, and those memories burn in our souls even when we deny them to the world. But we are inclined to see them as passing lapses into weakness and as insufficient to classify us among the ungrateful. We readily regard ourselves as justified in this because we do not think we have many acts of ingratitude with which to reproach ourselves.

Let's risk giving ourselves a third degree on this. In general, we do not think we number among the ungrateful. But are we not deceiving ourselves? The spirit of ingratitude in the world does not consist only in the fact that acts of ingratitude are committed but also in the fact that *too little appreciation is shown*. Granted that I can more or less absolve myself from acts of ingratitude, or at least think I can; can I also certify that everywhere I have had occasion to do so, I showed gratitude, or at least that I held myself ready to do so?

As soon as we throw light on the word "ingratitude" from both sides, our confidence is shaken. We all fail daily in that we soak up good deeds and friendly acts as sandy soil does water. And the desire to show ourselves thankful is not ordinarily the motivating power in our life. What the Apostle suggests in his marvelous words, "Be thankful in all things," has not permeated our minds yet. According to the standards that true morality demands of us, we all belong to the ranks of the ungrateful, even if we do not have that reputation in the world.

In order to clarify the general question Are you grateful? we must split it into two parts: Do you *feel* gratitude sufficiently? and Do you *show* gratitude sufficiently?

In order correctly to evaluate the first question—Do you feel gratitude sufficiently?—we must remind ourselves how often we have *become aware* of our need to show gratitude *only gradually,* not in the moment when we received something good. Later we are astonished that we did not recognize the meaning of the good deed and show our gratitude immediately.

None of us can think back to his youth without embarrassment, for we accepted so much then without a feeling of gratitude. It is painful to contemplate the graves of those who worked at our education or in some other equally selfless way that helped us go forward. They passed on without our having shown them what they were to us. We did not show them because we could not *evaluate* it, and we could not evaluate it because we did not *reflect upon* it. With increasing age, we have learned through experience better to appreciate things. But as for our imperfect sensitivity concerning acts of kindness we have received, we all, however gray-haired we have become, betray an incredible immaturity. We walk to and fro as dreamers and accept what others do for us as a matter of course when, in fact, it is anything but a matter of course. But we expect that others should treasure and bestir themselves over the least little thing that we ourselves do for them.

We all make the mistake of relying on our natural

sense of gratitude, and we assume this suffices to make us grateful people. This compares to true gratitude like the ears of grass to ears of wheat. Grass, too, has ears that bloom and produce kernels like wheat. But those poor kernels are not able to sustain our life, whereas those plants like wheat, which are improved and cultivated from the grasses, can do so. So likewise we must perfect and ennoble those natural feelings of gratitude that our life demands of us through *self-training*. If we fail to do so, it usually happens that our disposition supports us in the illusion that we really are grateful people.

Acquiring a sense of gratitude involves our taking nothing for granted, from whomever it may come and whatever it may be. Rather, we are to seek out the friendly intention behind the act and to appreciate it. Make a point of measuring every good deed that comes to you from other people according to its true worth. *Nothing that may befall you is self-evident.* Everything leads back to a will for good that is directed toward you.

If you try earnestly and constantly to train yourself in gratitude, you will have trouble with the stubborn person in you. When he expects appreciation, he shies like a foolish horse before a puddle. He always knows a way to debunk what he has received. There is no end to his tricks.

The commonest evasion by which he seeks to avoid this sense of gratitude runs like this: "The other person was only doing his duty." Thus, our sense of gratitude toward our closest neighbors is degraded, and we reach the sad point of accepting acts of kindness from those who are dearest to us without giving them the refreshment and encouragement they need. Is it not this lack of a feeling of gratitude toward our neighbors that is responsible for the estrangement and misunderstanding that can creep in between them and us? Therefore, leave it completely undecided in judging what anyone does to you in respect of how far the person who does you good fulfills a duty or not. Only his good intention toward you and his kindness in putting it into effect may come under consideration. The intention that presents the reality is what concerns you.

Beware also of a double trick the ungrateful person in you likes to use. If the service rendered to you is considerable, then he says, "Well, but that didn't cause the other person any great trouble." If he knows that the service did cause the other person great bother, he says, "Well, I didn't benefit that much from it." Out of inner anxiety about being indebted to someone, we behave as if we were haggling over prices in a shop. Do not *give in to* such behavior. Always *set the highest value on such service.* Every time someone does something for you, see it immediately from his standpoint as well as from your own.

Someone has done you a great service without much effort. Suppose he has helped you get a job by taking a stop somewhere to recommend you. Or suppose by chance he may have been in a position to help you with little trouble to himself. Perhaps even he did not suspect how much he was useful to you. You, however, must consider what it meant *for you* that in that moment he did this or that and must feel appropriately grateful to him forever.

If the value of the service to you is small, you must always consider that you cannot evaluate how difficult or how easy it was for the other person. Outwardly insignificant things often represent a considerable effort or mean an overcoming of serious obstacles. For instance, you request some information and receive a letter that provides it. The letter represents perhaps ten minutes' work. But the person who wrote it, because he is obliging, may be approached from all sides to write many such letters, or to do many errands. You owe him thanks not only for the letter he wrote for you or for the errand he ran for you but also for the fact that he is even willing to use time for those who need him that other people might use for relaxation. Perhaps he wrote the letter with your information to you at midnight or on Sunday afternoon. It has often occurred to me that precisely those people who are not ready to serve others are those who are least appreciative of the small services that are done for them. They know the work and sacrifice that go together with common friendship only at second hand.

While training yourself to be grateful, be careful that you don't just feel yourself bound for that which is visibly performed for you. Remember those thoughtful deeds that are inconspicuous or whose recollection might prove an embarrassment to you. Perhaps you were once in a situation in which someone had the upper hand on you because of some careless comment of yours or of something you forgot to do or of something he knew about you. He might have made things awkward for you or even have brought you into disgrace, but he did *not* do so. Now, of course, this is all in the past. But you must not forget what you owe him, even though it may be humiliating for you.

In this self-training in the feeling of gratitude, you are wholly *on your own*. Your family and friends will never pull you up short on the matter of gratitude, but will reinforce your self-delusion that you are already a very appreciative person. If they laugh at you for making so much of what this or that person has done for you and if you are no longer able to share your feelings with them because they will not understand your feelings, then you are on the right track.

Why does a string on a harp or a violin give out such a beautiful tone, whereas stretched out on a table it makes scarcely any noise? The sensitive sound box vibrates along with it. Thus, the good deeds you meet in the world will have a right and beautiful tone only when the resonance of a mind prepared to be grateful is present.

Do you *show* gratitude sufficiently? This second question leads you also into the path of self-training just as did the question of our feeling gratitude sufficiently. There is a coldness that affects the world because we do not show enough gratitude to those to whom we feel grateful. These then conclude that we are ungrateful, and they suffer thereby.

Why do we so often fail to express the gratitude we feel? From thoughtlessness and laziness! Our attention is not sufficiently focused on it. Of the ten lepers whom Jesus healed, only one came back to him to thank him. Were the other nine ungrateful? By no means! They may even have thought of him as warmly as did the other one and spoken of what he had done for them with deep emotion. But after they had shown themselves to the priests in Jerusalem and were able to go home, only one thought of first returning again to the Lord. The others went off to their villages. They forgot the obvious thing: expressing their thanks. We, too, do the same thing hundreds and hundreds of times, in matters both great and small.

Recently a nurse who cares for surgery patients told me: "Half of the patients on my ward leave without so much as a farewell to me." Are those who neglect that all ungrateful? Certainly not. But when the day of their release comes, they are so concerned with their departures, and so engrossed in their relatives who have come to pick them up, that they forget to thank the nurses unless they happen accidentally to cross paths. They are in too much of a hurry to look for her and to shake hands, and in the pressure of the moment they omit it because they have not trained themselves to say thank you.

Never postpone gratitude. Scripture says, "Never let the sun set on your anger." Let the same hold true for gratitude! Express it on the same day you feel it! A friend from the country has sent you some fruit. You are touched by the gift and decide "to write to him today." A week later he comes to town and you have not yet written to him. In the course of your conversation, he asks if the package has arrived, and for both parties, the heartfelt thanks become painful apologies.

During the war, many prisoners and wounded men received kindness from strangers, perhaps even from enemies. When the time came for parting from those people, they reassured them that they would never forget them. Those who had received help undertook to send their benefactors a letter at the first opportunity and later to remain in constant touch with them. Of a thousand letters so planned, scarcely a dozen are ever written. Then those distant benefactors complain bitterly that there was no gratitude. In reality, it is there in the others' hearts. But it is as if it did not exist, because it did not cause them to write a letter, even though they can find time each day to read three or four newspapers from beginning to end.

If we think seriously for just five minutes about where we have failed to show gratitude, the tormenting memories that come to mind must make us anxious and uneasy. How can we count the words and letters of gratitude left unsaid and unwritten, the personal visits we neglected?

Much was left undone because we forgot it. Other things we intended to do but put them off and never ever got around to doing them. Finally the occasion of gratitude lies so far in the past that we cannot return to it with good grace. Often, too, one whom we should like to thank has died before we get around to expressing our gratitude. Then to the pain of having lost him comes the additional sorrow of no longer being able to make good our ingratitude.

In still other cases, we have expressed our thanks to a person but had the opportunity years later to say to him once more that we still remember his kindness. But we pass it up. It is incredible how shyness, folly, carelessness, and indolence join forces with each other in order to make of us ungrateful people and how we are so careless and defenseless against their temptation. That is why we must train ourselves never to postpone the word or the visit to express gratitude and never to regard gratitude as completed, but, rather, later, as the opportunity arises, to let the other person know that it is still alive in us.

And just as there must be neither procrastination nor postponement in your gratitude, it must *never cease even if there are later intervening difficulties.*

Someone had done something kind for you. Afterward something comes between you through no fault of yours. He disagrees with your opinions or disapproves of your relationship with this or that person. He may even have done you some harm or alienated you by something he has done. It is hard to be at enmity with someone whom we have cared about. It is more difficult still when it is a person to whom we were bound in gratitude.

Anyone who has been through the experience of that in life knows the complications that arise in such a case. But no matter what happens, never say to yourself, *"I've had it with him!"* Allow the memory of the gratitude to survive everything that subsequently occurs, and when you find an occasion somehow to convey to him that, in spite of all, gratitude lives on in you, don't neglect to do so. Not even shyness about his possibly thinking ill of you or of his making fun of you may be allowed to hold you back. Reflect on what gratitude in its innermost being means: a human being *eternally joined to you* by mysterious bonds created by a deed done. He has a claim on you. Not a claim based in general laws such as he might expect but a claim granted by *you* and recognized and acknowledged by you. What this right demands of you, you must endeavor to give, wherever and whenever you can. The person to whom you owe a debt of gratitude may never be allowed to become just a person like any other to you; he remains someone special for you, like something that is holy to you.

II

Gratitude expressed through words and friendly acts is expected of us daily. Only in a small fraction of cases do we ever find ourselves in a situation of being able to show our indebtedness by acts that require considerable effort on our part. *To train ourselves duly to perform acts of gratitude* means taking up the battle against our lack of character and our love of comfort. With what pleasure and what dexterity we avoid acts of gratitude! Even the best among us possess a talent for self-deception that must cause them horror if they were to dare to admit it to themselves. To tally up the disappointments we have inflicted upon those who needed us and who had a claim upon our gratitude is devastating for each of us. Who does not see in his mind, indelibly, the eyes of those who have looked at us reproachfully? And often it was not a matter of great sacrifices that were required of us but services that we, with a little goodwill, might indeed have managed to perform.

Do not do as so many others around you do who only aim to be rid of these memories, yes, who even hate those people whom they have left in the lurch because they haunt them with humiliating memories. Experience that humiliation as something that has a strong and serious effect on what you will give in the future. Only he among us who in reflection upon his life has experienced horror and fear in the presence of his own ingratitude is capable of real gratitude.

It is important that you do not wait to show the gratitude you owe until the other person demands it from you. If you even suspect that he has need of help, come and offer it to him right away. Remember the situation where you have had to remind someone of his debt of gratitude to you and to beg some service of him. Those are the most difficult requests. Why don't we, wherever we can, spare each other those situations? Be sensitive and skillful in rendering gratitude. How often we humiliate and wound the other person who is obligated to us in such cases.

Be on guard, too, that your gratitude is not ruined because of fear of men. Many services we render as proof of our gratitude consist in some sort of advocacy for them. Perhaps we recommend them for something or vouch for them or take their side against slander or to protect them in case of injustice. Timidity and lack of character oppress you and give you excuses to avoid these duties. You would prefer, these feckless companions tell you, and could do, any other service. But it is not your duty to distinguish yourself by acting in this fashion, they say. Whatever use you could be to someone would be small, and compared to the misunderstandings and the unpleasantness you would expose yourself to, it would be absolutely nothing. In this and similar ways these two slick advocates talk. If you do not reject them under the influence of the first good impulse, they will bring you down. And when you have followed them once, they have you always in their power.

Note yet another thing in repaying gratitude. Do not even consider whether the service that now falls to you is greater than that which someone once did for you. Fate can require that for a small service you received you are to repay with a larger, perhaps even with a really large, service. Don't argue with fate. The same fate requires others who repay you for a small service to do so with a large service. Its ways are strange and defy scrutiny. Submit to them in giving as well as in receiving.

Standing the test of gratitude, however, is something more and broader than that upon occasion I help those people who have done some service for me. It consists in the fact that I *do* good simply because I have *received* good. Very often it is impossible to repay someone for what he has done for you. He may never be in a situation of needing your help, or perhaps he is even no longer in this world. Ordinarily one is not able to thank particular people for all the compassion you receive. Often you do not even know from whom it comes.

A man is brought into the Strasbourg hospital for surgery. Whom does he thank if he can be returned to health there? Not only the surgeon who performed the operation, the assistants who bandaged him, and the nurses who cared for him deserve his thanks but also the other people who stand in the background of past history. That there is a hospital there to take his case on at all goes back to those who founded it through their gifts. That he might be put gently to sleep and the operation not mean for him agonizing pain—which would have been the case a hundred years ago—comes to him as a gift from those who discovered ether and chloroform and from those who volunteered themselves to submit to the first tests of those stuffs. That one can now finally perform operations antiseptically, without the fear of infection that used to accompany all major surgery as a great danger, was bequeathed to him through the work of the Viennese physician Semmelweis. Semmelweis observed that all wound fevers are caused by invisible dirt that was introduced into the wound by the surgeon's hands. He also discovered that such can be avoided when the surgeon first disinfects his hands with disinfectant (Semmelweis first used chloride of lime, a bleaching powder). These benefactors from the past with whom he was not personally acquainted help in every operation, and the patient also owes his healing to them, without his ever being able to give them his gratitude. Thus he must do good to those who need it in their names.

Therefore *do good in gratitude* for the good from which you have benefited. Make your own tally and see if you are repaying the full amount you owe to unknown people and to fate itself. Have you been helped in time of illness? Then know that you must help someone else who is sick. Did someone make you a loan in your time of need? If you know someone else is in a similar situation, assist him in gratitude for what you have received. Did you go somewhere as a stranger, and did someone take you in? Then you should do the same for another stranger. Did someone run an errand for you or intercede for you? Then you must serve someone in the same way. Has someone helped you by giving you the right teaching to make something worthwhile of yourself? Look about and see if there isn't someone in equal need of your help. Have you been given without charge something for which one must usually pay? Then you must give something to someone for which you would ordinarily take payment. Has someone given time for you that he could scarcely afford to take? Then take time for another, even if you are overworked. This is what you must do all your life, in matters both great and small. Say little about it. It's a bookkeeping matter into which you alone can or ought to see. It is nobody else's business. Only be sure the balance is correct.

There are in nature certain plants that spread underground. The root grows in the soil under the surface and at intervals sends up new shoots into the air so that eventually several plants stand next to each other, apparently unconnected and independent of each other. In reality, however, they are gone out of the one common root that first grew there. That is also how good must spread. Let the kindness you receive send out fertile roots from which new acts of goodness may go forth. You must learn to understand the secret of gratitude. It is more than just a so-called virtue. It is revealed to you as a mysterious law of existence. In obedience to it we have to fulfill our destiny.

This is a mystical view of things. True. But whenever we penetrate to the bottoms of things, we always find something mysterious. Life and all that goes together with it is unfathomable. That which appears to belong to the commonplace takes on an unsuspectedly deep and consequential character when we analyze it thoroughly. Knowledge of life is recognition of the mysterious. To act justly means to obey the laws that arise from this recognition of the mysterious.

If you are striving to fulfill the great law of gratitude, the effort will bring you a notable ancillary blessing: You suffer much less from the ingratitude you meet than previously you did. Watch yourself in daily life and you will observe the hundreds of times you are remiss in showing gratitude. You will then not judge others as harshly as do those who have not undertaken such self-analyses. The feeling of guilt that burdens you will make you indulgent of others. You will have realized how difficult it is really to give thanks in all things and to all people. The failure of others to give you what you are owed will not hurt you so much as it did when you still naively got angry.

But beyond that, you know that there is more gratitude present in the world than meets the eye, for much felt gratitude never manages to come to words or deeds. You will comfort yourself with this thought when others are uncomprehending. The ingratitude in the world is a power of evil that no longer has its whole power over you. You can relinquish to the many thoughtless and ungrateful people the adage "Ingratitude is the reward you get from the world" as their booty. But as for yourself, you have learned to smile like one who has seen into things and behind things and does not stay with such sorry "wisdom."

AFTERWORD TO THE
FIRST EDITION

The twelve texts printed in this volume form a complete series of sermons that Schweitzer preached between February and August 1919 in Strasbourg's Saint Nicolai Church. At that time, as vicar, he was the only pastor there: "After the Armistice, through which Alsace left German administration and went over into French, I had to discharge the ministry at Saint Nicolai for a time completely on my own. Pastor Gerrold, who had been removed from his office by the German government for anti-German utterances, had not yet been reinstated by the French, and Pastor Ernst . . . had to give up his post for insufficiently French sentiments. . . ."

That this book is able to appear, that we—in addition to this selection—possess a great part of Schweitzer's sermons, at least in transcript, today at all, we owe to the care of Frau Emmy Martin, Schweitzer's coworker, and to his wife, Frau Helene Schweitzer. During the Second World War, Frau Annie Fischer-Stinnes (Stuttgart) undertook to prepare copies of the original manuscripts (of about one hundred fifty sermons). Frau Martin saved the main body of these transcripts by getting them to Günsbach, where they are preserved today in the central archives. The originals, and probably additional transcripts as well, were burned during a bombardment of Stuttgart.

In 1970, I also found, among the transcripts that had been brought to Günsbach, an index of all the sermons Schweitzer had preached and written down up to his first voyage out to Lambarene. The index—prepared by Helene Schweitzer—is very carefully supplied with sermon texts and dates, information from which one can determine when and where the sermons were preached. The number of sermons, the devotion and intensity of work that are reflected in them, are imposing. According to the index, Schweitzer prepared and wrote down some three hundred sermons and sketches. The people to whom Schweitzer gave his original manuscripts for the purpose of getting them transcribed are also noted.

That sermons 4 through 10 of the present volume can be printed is due to the agreement and the friendly assistance of Frau Emmy Martin, to whom Schweitzer had given the originals as keepsakes. We had been in contact with each other since 1930 and have exchanged many letters. During four long stays in Günsbach, then, I got acquainted with her kindness and the magnanimity of her character, as well as winning a deep look into her selfless life in matters of the "Doctor."

The constitution of the text and the commentary have been taken on by Lothar Stiehm. That the materials are so presented that when we read in the book we are simultaneously challenged to our own further work is due to him.

Together we thank Frau Rhena Schweitzer-Miller for her agreeing to the printing of the texts.

Wülfrath, Autumn 1973   MARTIN STREGE

DATE DUE			

Schweitzer   213951